How to Rebuild and Modify HIGH-PERFORMANCE Manual Transmissions

Paul Cangialosi

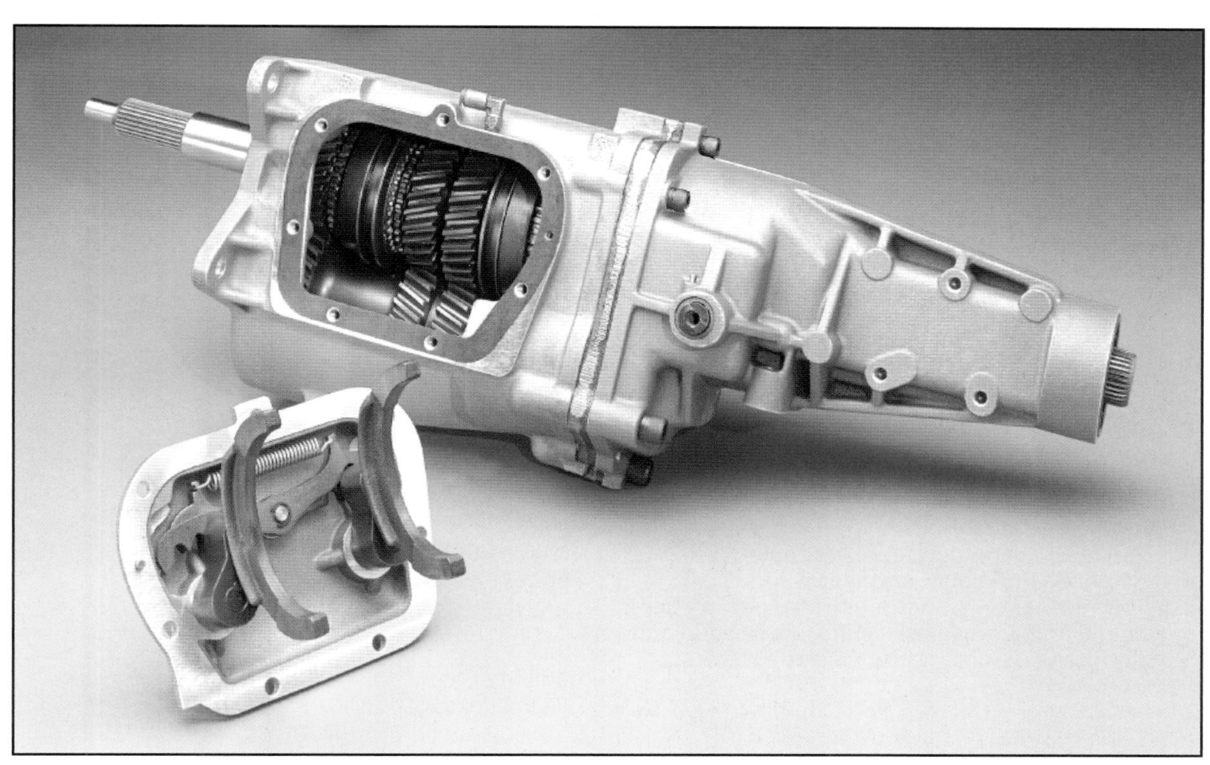

CarTech®

CarTech®

CarTech®, Inc.
6118 Main Street
North Branch, MN 55056
Phone: 651-277-1200 or 800-551-4754
Fax: 651-277-1203
www.cartechbooks.com

Edit by Paul Johnson
Layout by Monica Seiberlich

ISBN 978-1-934709-29-0
Item No. SA103

Library of Congress Cataloging-in-Publication Data
Cangialosi, Paul.
How to rebuild & modify high-performance manual transmissions / by Paul Cangialosi.
p. cm.
Previous ed. under title: How to build and modify high-performance manual transmissions.
ISBN 978-1-934709-29-0
1. Automobiles—Transmission devices. 2. Automobiles—Transmission devices—Maintenance and repair.
3. Automobiles—Performance. 4. Automobiles—Performance—Maintenance and repair. I. Cangialosi, Paul. How to build and modify high-performance manual transmissions. II. Title.
TL262.C36 2010
629.2'440288—dc22
2009029139

Written, edited, and designed in the U.S.A.
Printed in China
15 14 13 12 11

Cover:
The JT-5 on the left is a hybrid of the Tremec T-5. A new upgraded Muncie M22 "Rock Crusher" is on the right.

Title Page:
Auto Gear Equipment's new replacement M22 for the General Motors Muncie M22 4-Speed is shown.

Back Cover Photos
Top Left:
The power flow through the mainshaft and countershaft is shown in reverse gear.

Top Right:
Flip the synchro assembly over and install the second spring in a clockwise direction. When assembled, the springs will be opposite of one another and create a nice balance.

Middle Left:
Pre-lube the synchro rings in Dextron III fluid prior to installation. Install the second-gear ring set first.

Middle Right:
Once the counter gear has been placed back in the case, the upper geartrain is ready to be installed. This is my basic angle of approach to get the whole upper geartrain back in place.

Bottom Left:
Here is a nice cutaway of the TKO600. Unlike the T5 it has multiple shift rails.

Bottom Right:
McLeod Industries produces an extremely light multi-disc clutch and flywheel.

OVERSEAS DISTRIBUTION BY:
PGUK
63 Hatton Garden
London EC1N 8LE, England
Phone: 020 7061 1980 • Fax: 020 7242 3725
www.pguk.co.uk

Renniks Publications Ltd.
3/37-39 Green Street
Banksmeadow, NSW 2109, Australia
Phone: 2 9695 7055 • Fax: 2 9695 7355
www.renniks.com

Canada
Login Canada
300 Saulteaux Crescent
Winnipeg, MB, R3J-3T2 Canada
Phone: 800 665 1148 • Fax: 800 665 0103
www.lb.ca

CONTENTS

ACKNOWLEDGMENTS

I probably would not be writing this book if not for Fred Lewandowski. Fred allowed me, as a young teen, to channel my energy in a creative direction. He also gave me the best automotive education that no school could ever match. I never would have thought back then that my knowledge gained from working with this man would give me a lifetime career.

At an early age, my father taught me how to build model cars. He was an extraordinary model builder. Model building teaches patience, craftsmanship, pride in one's work, importance of reading instructions, and creative vision. For that, I thank you, Dad.

I blame Uncle Joe for his involvement in my addiction to manual transmissions. He allowed me to spend summers at his house reading car magazines and catalogs. I drove his 1965 Falcon Sprint (a 4-speed, of course), up and down his driveway, which subsequently led to my first clutch installation, shifter adjustment, and initiation to the smell of gear lube.

I thank my mother and grandparents for enduring years of transmission parts and disassembled autos scattered across the backyard and sometimes on the kitchen table. How did they ever put up with it?!

My wife, Cora, has stood by my side and also has had to endure a missing husband for countless days, nights, and sometimes weeks. It is only through her strength and conviction in me that I am able to write this book. Although I have an editor for this book, Cora has become the editor for my life.

I also thank the late Steve Hendrickson and CarTech Books for believing in me. He made a life-long dream come true.

I thank Brian Higgins of SK Speed for his countless hours aiding me with parts, statistics, and his life's knowledge.

There are so many new acquaintances and friends that have developed as a result of this project. Thank you for your time, knowledge, and belief in me.

Shift Fast,
Paul Cangialosi

PREFACE

My first introduction into the workings of a transmission and why one is needed came with the acquisition of my first bicycle. It was a 20-inch single-speed bike. I could only pedal to a point, at which no matter how fast I pedaled, acceleration flattened out. I was able to achieve a higher "top end" by changing out the pedal sprocket to one with a larger diameter. However, this made my initial acceleration suffer. My uncle Joe had this "English Racer" bicycle, which we children were instructed never to touch. It had five speeds! With the help of some tools and extra hubs, I was able to stick his sprocket assemblies on my 20-inch bike. This new sprocket arrangement gave me the acceleration and top end I needed, and it was probably the fastest 20-inch bike in town. This was my first introduction to the importance of gearing and transmissions.

My journey into this madness started in the late 1970s. An "A-level Journeyman" taught me how to repair engines and automatic transmissions. Four-speeds, back then, were only in hot rods or muscle cars, so as a general repair mechanic I rarely saw them. When one did finally surface for repair, I was hooked. I think the physical aspect sets building and repairing these types of transmissions apart from automatics. The end user has to shift it physically. That person's enjoyment or frustration of his or her shifting experience is directly related to how well you build the transmission. In fact, each time a person pulls a clean, smooth shift, he or she may be actually thinking of how great a job the rebuilder did.

Over a course of 27 years, I've met many people with the same addiction toward gears, and interestingly, there are not that many. I estimate there are fewer than 30 people in the United States who specialize in manual transmissions alone, and probably no more than 15 who do it on a full-time basis. Most are still hobbyists and work a full-time job for real income. Some stick to one type of transmission and become specialists in that particular design. There are others who specialize in doing modifications, such as making lightweight 2-speeds out of 4-speeds for circle-track racing. It starts by accumulating mass quantities of similar transmissions. It is not uncommon for a transmission specialist to have a few hundred of the same gearbox. It takes years of building and collecting parts to actually decipher what types of castings, ratios, and even hardware were used in the production of certain makes and models. Gear manufacturing in the United States doesn't exist on a large scale anymore. Major car manufacturers purchase the bulk of standard-shift transmissions from Mexico, Japan, and Germany. Corvettes and Mustangs all use Mexican-made transmissions. There are fewer than 10 specialty shops in this country that actually design and build new high-performance or racing components for this market today.

The original concept of this book was based on a smaller manual I called *Setting Standards*. Released in the late 1980s, it mainly provided answers to common questions related to transmissions. These questions came from 14-plus car shows that I attended every year. What I gathered was that there is a certain type of person who is drawn to manual-shift transmissions. It could be the smell of 90wt gear lube or the attraction of mechanical components working together. I also noticed that most automatic transmission or engine builders rarely venture into manual-transmission territory. The precision setup of a geartrain can be intimidating. So, the goal of this book is to break down the mystique of the gearbox. This book will help you understand design concepts, theory, building techniques, and history of the manual-shift transmission. If you decide to purchase or rebuild a standard transmission the explanations set forth here should aid you in making better choices and build confidence.

Today's internal combustion engine requires a transmission to effectively transmit power. Electric motors or steam engines do not. These get power from an outside source. Using steam or electricity to power them, they can generate torque at zero rpm. Also, both steam engines and electric motors can easily operate in reverse direction without the use of a transmission. This cannot be easily accomplished with an internal combustion engine. If you try putting a load on a typical gasoline engine at very low RPM, it will stall. When most people first learn to drive with a manual-shift transmission, they usually stall out the engine until the technique of slipping the clutch is mastered. Getting back to riding a 5-speed bicycle, I always tell people to associate your legs as being the engine. It will be very easy to start off in first gear. Your legs won't have to work as hard. You may be able to start off in fifth gear, but you have to work very hard to initially start. The extra work of starting in fifth gear eventually strains and fatigues your legs. The same is true for an engine. When a high gear is selected at low RPM, the engine lugs in that gear because it is overworked. Lugging causes unwanted wear and tear on engine components. So what you learn is that even though a transmission is required, the proper use of gear ratios for a specific application is just as important.

Manual transmissions today are far more complex than those built in the 1950s or 1960s. The objective of this book is to touch on high-performance transmissions. Most high-performance transmissions today are based on the older rear-wheel-drive designs. This simple design incorporates an input shaft and an output shaft that attaches to a driveshaft that spins your rear axle.

You may hear the term "transaxle." Transaxles, mounted in the rear of the car, incorporate a transmission and rear axle gearing as a complete unit. Tremec's T56 6-speed came as a standard rear-wheel-drive transmission in the Camaro, but it was a transaxle in the Corvette. A front-wheel-drive axle does the opposite. The transmission and final drive are mounted in the front, and axles drive the front wheels.

Many cars are now equipped with all-wheel drive. All-wheel drives are usually computer controlled to give optimum traction and power to the wheel that needs it the most. All-wheel drive should not be confused with 4-wheel drive. Typical, 4-wheel-drive (4x4) vehicles, such as a Jeep for example, use a conventional rear-wheel-drive transmission with a "transfer case" bolted to the back of it. The transfer case then sends power to the front wheels and also act as a link to the rear wheels.

The basic manual-shift transmission has an input shaft, countergear, speed gears, and an output shaft. Typically, power comes into the input shaft, goes down through the countergear, then up to a speed gear and out through the output shaft. Selection of a particular gear is accomplished by locking the speed gear to the output shaft. The number of speed gears in a transmission determines if the transmission is a 3-speed, 4-speed, 5-speed, etc. Each pair of gears in a transmission is called a set. Each set can have a specific gear ratio. One turn of the drive gear in the set can create multiple turns, one turn, or fewer than one turn of the driven gear. This is the basis of a gear ratio. The difference between one gearset's ratio as opposed to another is called a "spread" or "drop." This is expressed as a percentage.

After dealing with many mechanics and transmission shops over the years, many people still don't understand what a gear ratio is, how it is calculated, and how important proper use of ratios are. Gear ratios can be used in different operational modes. The modes are underdrive, overdrive, direct, reverse, and neutral. In underdrive mode, the input spins more than the output. In overdrive mode, the output spins more than the input. In direct mode, both input and output are either locked together or the overall ratio is 1:1. Neutral allows both input and output to be independent of one another. Reverse causes the output to spin in the opposite direction of the input and is always an underdrive ratio. We determine gear ratios by using simple division and multiplication.

This book focuses on high-performance manual transmissions. The transmissions overviewed in this book are based on current popularity as well as historical demand for parts and service. There are no 3-speed transmissions featured because they are no longer considered a high-performance transmission. Light-duty 4-speeds, such as the GM Saginaw, have been omitted from the build section as well.

The transmissions I decided to include were ones that I'm asked about every day. Manual transmissions pretty much function in the same way. The cases and size of the gears may change, but the basic principles are very similar. Therefore, I included chapters on theory as well as common rebuilding techniques that apply to most of them. If a transmission is not overviewed in this book, you should be able to use these basic procedures to tackle most transmission jobs.

A brief history of each make and model is given. This is not meant to be a restorer's guide; however, certain popular models have more historical data as well as ID information.

Shifters and clutch information is included because they are something you will have to address when working on your transmission. To help round out your newfound knowledge of manual transmissions, I included a chapter on high-end race transmissions rarely seen or discussed in most publications.

Although this book should answer most of your questions regarding building manual transmissions, support for any additional information can be obtained online. Just go to the support forums at www.5speeds.com.

INTRODUCTION

You should congratulate yourself for investing in this book. In this time when people expect free information from the Internet, fewer and fewer people are investing in comprehensive information found in manuals and books that make complete buildups possible. Professional repair shops as well as individuals for some odd reason no longer feel they have to purchase overhaul manuals for cars or individual components they need to work on. Every workday includes a few phone calls to me from people who purchased the wrong transmission, wrong parts or got misinformation from the Internet. A great deal of research went into this publication. That research is based on 25 years in this business as well as interacting with some of the best people in the standard transmission field.

A great number of transmissions produced in the 1940s to late 1950s shared similar design concepts. More cars are mass-produced today than in the 1940s, and it is interesting to note that there are more surplus gears still sitting on shelves for transmissions made during the 1940s and 1950s. The reason is that they broke more often, and spare parts were incorporated into the design concept.

During the 1960s through the end of the 1970s, the manual-shift transmission business was hot. There was a great deal of horsepower being generated, and transmissions were not holding up to abuse that well. The OEM (Original Equipment Manufacturers) spent the first part of this decade improving on their original designs to accept the increasing horsepower levels. If you were involved with gearbox building during this time, you witnessed first hand how changes in castings or alloys altered strength. The significant designs created at this time are still the foundation for today's transmissions. I've taken a great deal of time to contact friends in the industry and speak to builders who are "in the know" to help document some of these changes.

By 1975 catalytic converters and lower horsepower levels started to prevail, and the OEM no longer had to accept responsibility for broken transmissions. If you purchased a Corvette in 1975 that had an advertised 190 hp and decided to modify the engine to make 375 hp, it was now your problem if you exploded the transmission. The period from 1975 to 1982 is what I call the "dry period." This was a time during which the aftermarket and OEMs did very little. The cost to design and manufacture new gears or castings was extremely high and limited only to a few shops. The economic recession in the U.S. didn't help matters as well. Most of the shops that did work for the OEM in the past also did the bulk of the professional race work for NASCAR and sanctioned drag race organizations.

By 1983 the IBM PC started to change the way people worked. Computer Aided Design (CAD) programs started to find there way into smaller machine shops. This was the start of "New Design Period." Many new designs were created and tweaked out during this period. Newer style alloys, new ways to form gear teeth as part of a forging process, and the use of friction paper in synchro rings instead of traditional bronze were developed. Powdered metal processes and strong computer-designed die-cast cases were some of the advances. This period from 1983 to 1996 represents a time in which software designers were able to give engineers better tools to improve reliability, gas mileage and incorporate fewer components.

We are currently in the "high-tech period." By 1996 3D modeling software started to also become affordable, and this empowered a designer to truly see his vision. You can now look at your design concept from various angles, throw all sorts of "what if" data around, and thus create a more stable design. Once again, cars are now producing impressive power levels and are able to meet emissions requirements. This has resulted in new demand for aftermarket transmission parts. It seems that improving product reliability is no longer a priority for the

OEMs and larger manufacturers. Each year when I go to the Performance Racing Industry show, I notice that the bigger manufacturers seem to have the same old designs and have very few people interested in what they have to offer. In contrast, there is usually another company with just two employees actually designing and building much more sophisticated transmissions. Needless to say, their booths are overcrowded.

Every week someone asks me if I have any NOS (new old stock) gears. They have a hard time embracing new technology. For some odd reason they do not believe transmission technology has improved in 30 years. In fact, the quality of steels related to gears and bearings has greatly improved because the alloys are more consistent and pure. Gears are now machined more accurately than equivalent parts produced 40 years ago. A small shop now can produce a quality piece that exceeds anything a major manufacturer made in 1960.

The future of the manual-transmission business is based on the past. When researching how many new companies have started up in this field over the past 10 years, I was shocked to see that only a few have survived. Some die off quick simply because they don't have the foundation of the older technology. I've witnessed first hand how horrible gearbox designs fail because they are based on software rather than instinctual knowledge. The modern gearbox now has a computer or brain, and the brain is supposed to shift for you. Maybe this is a necessity in Formula 1 racing; however, it seems to me that we are taking the fun out of driving and also are redefining what the term "manual shift" means! So consider this a purist's book. I won't bore you with computer ECM troubleshooting, solenoid resistances, or places to plug your laptop in.

What is a *Workbench*® Book?

This Workbench® Series book is the only book of its kind on the market. No other book offers the same combination of detailed hands-on information and revealing color photographs to illustrate transmission rebuilding. Rest assured, you have purchased an indispensable companion that will expertly guide you, one step at a time, through each important stage of the rebuilding process. This book is packed with real world techniques and practical tips for expertly performing rebuild procedures, not vague instructions or unnecessary processes. At-home mechanics or enthusiast builders strive for professional results, and the instruction in our Workbench® Series books help you realize pro-caliber results. Hundreds of photos guide you through the entire process from start to finish, with informative captions containing comprehensive instructions for every step of the process.

Appendixes located in the back of the book provide essential specification and rebuild information.

The step-by-step photo procedures also contain many additional photos that show how to install high-performance components, modify stock components for special applications, or even call attention to assembly steps that are critical to proper operation or safety. These are labeled with unique icons. These symbols represent an idea, and photos marked with the icons contain important, specialized information.

Here are some of the icons found in Workbench® books:

Important!—Calls special attention to a step or procedure, so that the procedure is correctly performed. This prevents damage to a vehicle, system, or component.

Save Money—Illustrates a method or alternate method of performing a rebuild step that will save money but still give acceptable results.

Torque Fasteners—Illustrates a fastener that must be properly tightened with a torque wrench at this point in the rebuild. The torque specs are usually provided in the step.

Special Tool—Illustrates the use of a special tool that may be required or can make the job easier (caption with photo explains further).

Performance Tip—Indicates a procedure or modification that can improve performance. Step most often applies to high-performance or racing applications.

Critical Inspection—Indicates that a component must be inspected to ensure proper operation of the engine.

Precision Measurement—Illustrates a precision measurement or adjustment that is required at this point in the rebuild.

Professional Mechanic Tip—Illustrates a step in the rebuild that non-professionals may not know. It may illustrate a shortcut, or a trick to improve reliability, prevent component damage, etc.

Documentation Required—Illustrates a point in the rebuild where the reader should write down a particular measurement, size, part number, etc. for later reference or photograph a part, area or system of the vehicle for future reference.

Tech Tip—Tech Tips provide brief coverage of important subject matter that doesn't naturally fall into the text or step-by-step procedures of a chapter. Tech Tips contain valuable hints, important info, or outstanding products that professionals have discovered after years of work. These will add to your understanding of the process, and help you get the most power, economy, and reliability from your transmission.

THEORY OF MANUAL TRANSMISSIONS

Power flow in neutral.

Power flow in first gear.

Whether you are dealing with sprocket teeth on a bike or gear teeth on a transmission gear, the simple formula for calculating a gear ratio is: Ratio = Driven ÷ Drive.

So if the drive gear has 10 teeth and the driven gear 20 teeth, the ratio equals 2. This is expressed as a 2:1 or a 2.00 ratio. The drive gear must make two turns to make the driven gear turn once. Any ratio with a number greater than 1 is an underdrive ratio. A ratio less than 1 becomes an overdrive ratio. If the drive gear has 40 teeth and the driven has 30, the ratio becomes .75. This is expressed as.75:1. Sometimes overdrive ratios are expressed as a percentage. If the ratio is .75, the difference between .75 and 1.0 is .25 or 25 percent. Therefore, a .75 overdrive ratio is often called a 25 percent overdrive.

Because the average manual-shift transmission contains more than one pair of gears, the same formula holds true for each drive and driven set. The ratio of each drive and driven set is multiplied by each other to give the final ratio. The formula is:

Ratio =
(Driven ÷ Drive) x (Driven ÷ Drive)

Power flow in second gear.

Power flow in third gear.

Power flow in fourth or direct gear.

When looking at the nearby power-flow pictures for first-gear mode, you see that the power comes into the input shaft (drive), down to the countergear (driven), then from the countergear (drive) to the first-speed gear (driven). You can now figure your overall gear ratio. Here is an example: Your input shaft has 21 teeth. The mating driven section of the countergear has 25 teeth. The first-gear section of the countergear has 17 teeth, and the first-speed gear has 36 teeth. Using the formula:

$$\text{Ratio} = (25 \div 21) \times (36 \div 17) = 1.19 \times 2.12 = 2.52$$

Your first-gear ratio is 2.52:1.

Gear ratios are a very important aspect of transmission selection and transmission design. Ratios can help determine proper application as well as the torque capacity of a transmission. Two areas often overlooked when selecting a transmission are gear ratio and center-to-center distance.

The center-to-center distance is the distance between the centerlines of the upper and lower geartrains. To help visualize why a center-to-center distance is important, here is an extreme example: You can have two gearsets. Both sets have a 20-tooth driven gear and a 10-tooth drive gear; however, one set has a center-to-center of 1 inch while the other has a center-to-center of 3½ inches. The set with the larger center-to-center obviously has larger teeth and bigger gears. This yields a stronger transmission, but with a heavy geartrain. The transmission with the small center-to-center may shift easier, because of the lighter mass of the geartrain, but it will be weaker.

Power flow in fifth gear.

Power flow in reverse.

These two gears both have the same tooth count, but the one on the left is a larger-diameter shaft than the one on the right. The larger-diameter shaft has more surface area and, therefore, can transmit more power than the smaller-diameter shaft.

The proper selection of a transmission for a particular application is based on this idea. Thus, a car with a 150-hp engine that weighs 1,800 pounds would be robbed of performance if the engine had to turn a transmission designed for a 600-hp 3,000-lb vehicle.

Torque capacity seems to be the latest buzz word. Published torque ratings of transmissions are often misleading as well as misunderstood. As mentioned above, longer center-to-center distances improve capacity. Gear ratios affect capacity in several ways. A 3:1 ratio compared to a 2:1 ratio along the same center-to-center distance is usually weaker, by the nature of gear design. Fewer teeth are needed to obtain a larger reduction. A smaller-diameter gear with fewer teeth is weaker than a larger-diameter gear with more teeth.

There are some trade offs. The more teeth you put on a gear within a fixed diameter, the finer the pitch of that gear. This finer pitch results in a gear-tooth profile with a thinner cross section in contrast to a gear of the same diameter with fewer teeth. You can actually improve the strength of the gear by giving it a bigger diameter with fewer teeth. In mass-produced transmissions, the manufacturer very rarely makes a separate profile for each gearset. That is what the specialty performance shops do.

So what does a published rating of 300 ft-lbs of torque really mean? A torque rating is not a static rating.

This means you don't stick a breaker bar and lock the transmission in two gears and apply 300 ft-lbs of torque to the input shaft and watch something snap when you exceed the 300 pounds. Consider a torque rating as a life factor of a transmission based on a particular application.

After speaking in depth to various engineers from several manufacturers regarding this issue, I've come to the conclusion that you can think of a torque rating as being a dynamic rating based on a theoretical life factor. For example, let's say we feel a transmission should yield good service for 100,000 miles in a car that has an engine that produces 300 ft-lbs of peak torque. Obviously, the transmission is never seeing that engine's peak torque all the time. Actually, unless you have no rear axle, the torque coming out of the engine is absorbed by both transmission and rear axle. In fact, a dead rear-axle ratio, such as a 3.08 rear, will cause the transmission to load more than a 4.11 rear.

You can exceed the rating of the transmission but you will shorten the transmission's life factor. The rating is actually a safe benchmark. Different manufacturers arrive at published ratings using different methods of calculations, making it really impossible to compare one transmission to another.

The Tremec T5 5-speed originally designed by BorgWarner had its published ratings actually change when Tremec took over the line. The T5s have their published ratings exceeded every day. The ones that survive probably have better rear-axle gearing, such as a 4.11. Transaxles designed for the 24 Hours of LeMans race are loaded on a dyno to simulate real-life loads against engines producing more than 1,000 hp. They are designed to last for that one race. I prefer real-world applications and factual data as opposed to hypothetical data any day. So keep an open mind when asking about or reading published ratings.

Today, more and more people are swapping various engines and transmissions into custom projects. Few take the time to understand these basic principles. Much energy, time, and money are wasted trying to adapt Toyota Supra transmissions to Jaguars or 4-cylinder S-10 Truck 5-speeds to a 1968 Camaro. I am asked these "Will it work?" questions every week. In some parts of the world, certain transmissions are more readily available than others. Australia has an over abundance of Toyota 5-speeds, thus people are always trying to stick them into everything in sight. The point is to save time and money by selecting the proper application for a project.

Wide- and Close-Ratios Explained

What does having a wide- or close-ratio manual-shift transmission mean? First of all, it has nothing to do with how close or wide your shifter moves within its pattern. That is called having a "long- or short-throw" shifter. I'll discuss here a simple method that will show what close and wide ratio is.

There is no particular formula that determines whether you have a close- or wide-ratio gearbox. I say this because what was considered wide ratio in the 1960s is considered close ratio today. Confused? Since you now know what a gear ratio is, the difference between two gear ratios is called a ratio spread or drop. That drop is a percentage of the previous ratio. Here is a formula to calculate that change:

$$\text{Percentage Drop} = (\text{Ratio 1} - \text{Ratio 2}) \div \text{Ratio 1}$$

For example, let's say we have a close-ratio 4-speed Super T10. The ratios are: 2.64 first, 1.61 second, 1.23 third, and 1.00 fourth.

$$(2.64-1.61) \div 2.64 = .390$$
$$(1.61-1.23) \div 1.61 = .236$$
$$(1.23-1.00) \div 1.23 = .186$$

Rounding up a bit, you can see that the ratio change between the gears is: 39 percent, 24 percent, and 19 percent.

BorgWarner's extra-low-ratio Super T10 had a 2.88 first, 1.75 second, 1.33 third and 1:00 fourth. If you plug these gear ratios into the above formula, you end up with the following drop: 39 percent, 24 percent, and 25 percent.

Think of gear ratios as a distance between two points. In a typical muscle car, 4-speed application fourth gear is direct, or 1:1 ratio. Again, thinking in terms of distance, consider fourth gear or direct as your final destination. The further you get away from 1:1 (direct) the wider the ratio.

The Muncie M21 and M22 close-ratio 4-speeds were the closest ratio 4-speeds ever put into a production car. Their ratios were 2.20 first, 1.64 second, 1.28 third, 1:00 fourth. If you plug those ratios into the formula, you end up with 25 percent, 22 percent, and 22 percent.

Compare these percentage drops to the previous drops found using the Super T10. Notice that although the

2-3 and 3-4 drops of the Super T10 and Muncie are pretty close percentage-wise, but the 1-2 drops vary quite a bit. The reason is that the Super T10s have a lower (higher numerical) first gear. The 2.88 and 2.64 ratios are further away from direct than the Muncie's 2.20 first-gear ratio.

What Makes a Close-Ratio Close?

As you have learned, you can't gain distance without losing closeness. The lower the first gear, the wider the 4-speed will be. If one takes a historical look at the close-ratio gearbox, it usually had 25 percent or lower drops across all gear spreads. The problem is: the Muncie close-ratio box was designed in the 1960s when we really didn't worry much about gas mileage. In order for you to get a "close ratio," a Muncie-equipped car had at least a 3.70 rear-end gear. You needed at least that low of a final drive to get your car moving. The "wide ratio" M20 had a 2.52 first gear. You could get a 3.31 or 3.55 rear with that gear and gain a little more economy, but it wasn't cool to have what was considered a wide-ratio box in your Corvette.

By late 1974, fuel economy and air pollution became considerations, and catalytic converters were mandatory by 1975. Axle ratios had to drop to get the improved gas mileage the Environmental Protection Agency (EPA) demanded. So in order to get cars moving with 3.08 or 2.88 rear-end gears, cars that had engines with decent amounts of low-end torque were equipped with "close-ratio" transmissions. Larger engines carried transmissions with 2.64 first gears while smaller-displacement engines' first-gear ratios were in the 3.0 range. So the newer close-ratio transmissions are actually wider than the older wide- and close-ratio transmissions!

Doug Nash Corporation had an interesting solution to this dilemma. It developed a 5-speed box with a close-ratio spread like a Muncie M21 with a fifth-gear direct. Again, think about "distance between two points." The more stops you make in your travel to get to your final destination, the closer the distance between your stops. By adding a lower first-speed gear and keeping a direct fifth, you gain more distance, but add an extra stop. The Doug

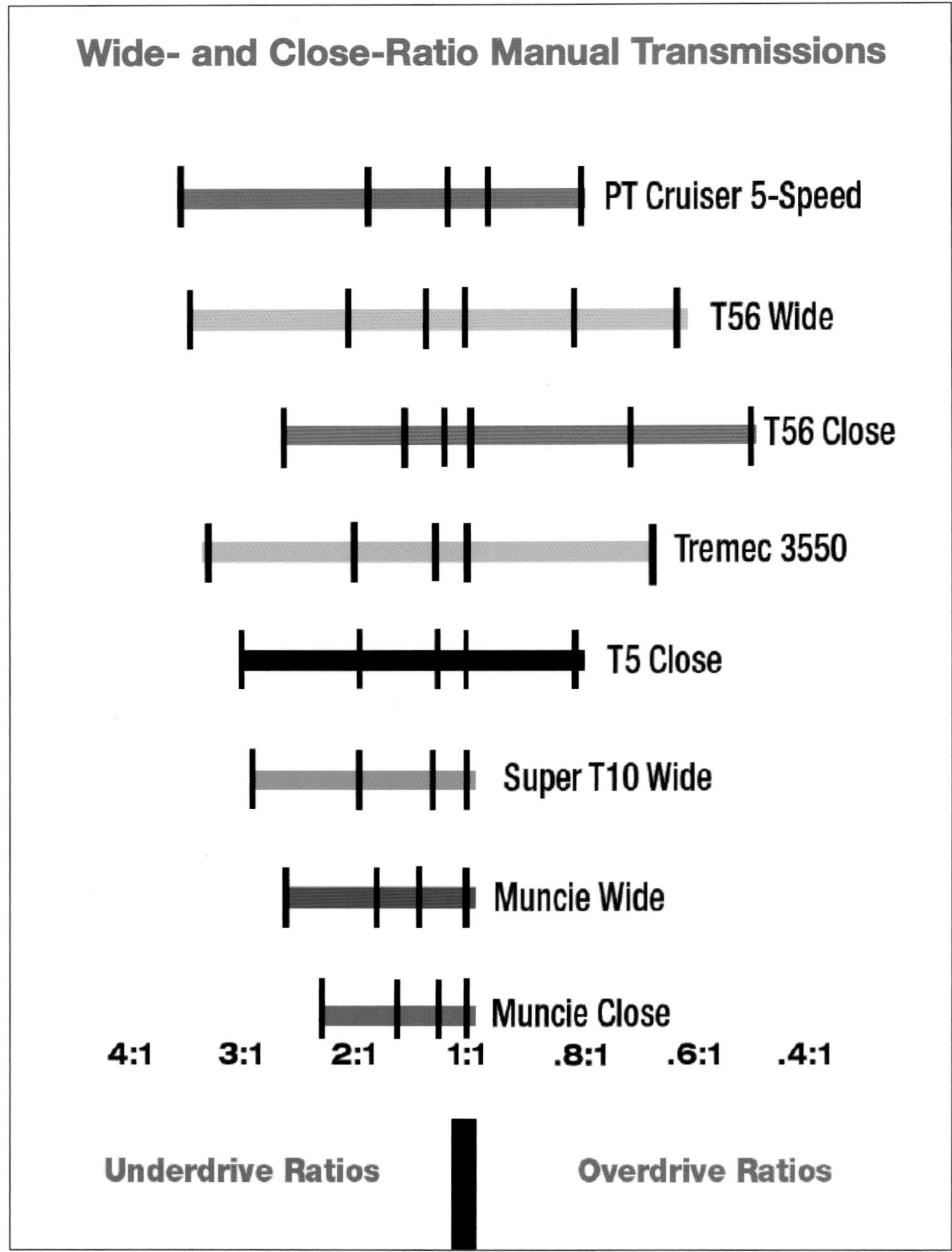

This chart shows different ratios of popular manual gearboxes. The Muncie M21 and M22 close-ratio provide the narrowest range of gear ratios while the T56 provides the widest range of ratios through the gears.

Nash Street 5-speed came with a 3.27 first gear. This allowed drag enthusiasts to use a 3.08 final drive and still get good close-ratio acceleration. It worked great.

Today, cars produce a great deal of low-end torque. Most peak power is made in the 4,500-rpm range. The average 5-speed, such as a T5, is an extremely wide ratio by 1960s standards. The close-ratio T5s used by Ford Motorsport have a 2.95 first, 1.94 second, 1.34 third, 1.00 fourth, and .80 fifth. You do the math with the formula. These new 5- and 6-speeds, in a sense, are really wide-ratio 4-speeds with additional overdrive gears for fifth and sixth speed. Cars can now cruise at 1,800 rpm at 70 mph because the engine's torque curve can handle the load. If you are still thinking in terms of distance, not only are you getting further away from our final destination of direct drive, but you are now going past your final destination into two levels of overdrive.

Chrysler's PT Cruiser has a 2.4L 150-hp 4-cylinder engine. The engine produces 162 ft-pounds at 4,000 rpm, and the 5-speed transaxle has a final drive of 3.94! The first ratio is 3.50, second is 1.96, third is 1.36, fourth is .97, and fifth is .81. This is really a 3-speed with two overdrive ratios. The engine doesn't produce power until it hits 4,000 rpm. Thus, the gearing sort of works, but the car can be boggy at lower RPM.

Goodbye Wide- and Close-Ratios

The chart on page 14 shows shift points of some popular transmissions. For the most part, cars are no longer offered with close- or wide-ratio transmission options. If you look at the chart, you see that by plotting stops of a distance traveled, you realize what close or wide ratio may mean. In one sense, if you compare stops, some transmissions have similar distances between one or two stops while others are drastically different. What is close or wide ratio is no longer an issue. Rather, how much percentage drop your engine can handle is the issue.

Road racing events, such as NASCAR- or SCCA-type races, still require transmissions with a close-ratio spread. It is common for some of these cars to have 1.86 first-gear ratios. Plot a gearbox on the chart on page 14 with a 1.86 first, 1.59 second, 1.17 third, and 1.00 fourth. How do those results look in comparison to the others? What percentage drops does that same box create using the formula?

In our example, a low first gear is not needed because road race cars tend to operate at the higher range of RPM and speed with no stopping other than for a pit stop. An ultra-close-ratio gearbox has other advantages as well. Since the load changes are not as severe, drivetrain parts tend to live longer. The high-shock loads of wide-ratio transmissions usually cause gearbox failure and rear-axle failure.

Less heat is generated in a close-ratio box. A car having a final drive of 2.98 and a direct fourth gear has the same overall ratio as a car with a .80 overdrive fifth and 3.73 final drive. The car with the overdrive uses more horsepower and generates more heat through the transmission than the direct-drive box. However, the 3.73 rear may offer more low-speed punch on turns.

My point here is that when it comes to what is right for your car, it is still a matter of trial and error.

Getting your street or race car geared properly produces fantastic results. Jerico, G-Force, and Liberty's all make excellent 4- and 5-speed gearboxes for drag-race applications. If you have a track-only car, then sticking a 4.11 or 4.56 rear-end gear and using a 4- or 5-speed race gearbox will produce better results than any street 5-speed. When it comes to road racing, find other people using similar engine and rear combinations to yours. Compare how they do against one another, especially if they use a different transmission.

The How and Why of Synchros

Historically, manual transmissions were defined as either progressive or selective. When you shift a transmission, you are disengaging one gear from the mainshaft (also called the output shaft) and engaging another. A progressive transmission has one massive gearset with one shifting mechanism. When you shift you mate this single one-piece set to various gears on the countergear assembly. Thus, it has one lever. A selective transmission has individual gears that are locked to the output. A typical 4-speed transmission has three levers, one lever each for 1-2, 3-4, and reverse. How you make the transition from one gear to another is accomplished by sliding one gear into another by use of a synchronizer.

"Sliding gear technology," as I call it, is often misunderstood. Today, very few transmissions use sliding gears, but any old 4-speed still uses a sliding non-synchro reverse gear. The later T5 5-speeds used a sliding reverse and then a synchronized reverse brake. I sell more reverse gearsets because people see chipped teeth and think they need to be replaced. In many cases, they probably don't need to be replaced and will be chipped within a few months anyway. A sliding gear has no way of stopping the gear it is being mated to, so it will usually grind and chip the leading edges. What most people don't realize is that the gear, when fully engaged, over-hangs the mating gear. The edge that initially contacts the mating gear slides past it and overhangs on the back side, while the mating gear overhangs on the front side. Consequently, this area is designed to be chipped! Usually, if the gear is chipped no more than one-quarter of the way, the gear will be fine.

Synchronizers make sure the selected gear is locked to the output shaft at the same speed so no grinding occurs. Every performance manual-shift transmission that uses synchronizers follows these rules:

Leading edges of gears chip, but then overhang once the gears are engaged.

- All gears are in constant mesh; this means that they don't need to slide into one another. They are, in fact, already spinning as a matched set.
- Although the gears are in constant mesh, they are floating on the output shaft.
- The synchronizer is always locked to the output shaft.
- The synchronizer's job is to lock a particular gear to the output shaft, so power can now flow through the gear and out of the shaft.

Understanding theory, components, and operation of the manual transmission is the key to successfully diagnosing problems. Many people think they know how synchros work, but usually misdiagnose because of a poor understanding of the theory. Let's see if we can resolve this mystery once and for all.

Synchronize, as defined by Webster's Dictionary is "to cause to move, operate or work at the same rate and exactly together." In fact, you are trying to get a speed gear to operate at the same RPM as the mainshaft so you can lock it to the shaft without any hint of a grind in the split-second called a "shift." The synchronizer (or synchro) in a common performance transmission is made up of a hub, slider (also called a clutch), strut keys, springs, and synchro rings (also called blocker rings). The hub is splined to the output shaft. The slider is the sliding component that physically mates the speed gear to the hub, thus locking the speed gear to the mainshaft. In the process of moving the slider to engage the selected gear, strut keys track with the slider and exert pressure on the synchro ring. In turn, the gear slows down to allow the slider and gear to couple.

The synchro pictures on pages 10 to 12 show several important aspects of synchro design. They show how a synchro ring relates to the gear on the upshift in contrast to the downshift.

During the upshift, as the slider moves toward the selected gear, the slider's keys exert pressure on the ring, which tries to lock onto that gear. The drag of the ring against the cone of the gear forces the ring to wind up in the same direction the gear is moving.

The struts have a two-fold purpose. The first is to apply pressure to the ring so that it can lock on the gear and the second is to "index" the ring. Proper synchro indexing is the ticket to a clean and effortless shift.

Note that the ring must move in the opposite direction in order for the slider to pass through. When you shift, you press down on the clutch pedal, which temporarily uncouples the transmission from the engine. Once uncoupled, the gear can slightly "blip" in the opposite direction and complete the shift.

It's important to realize that the complete gearset is in constant mesh. As a result, the inertia of all the gears—not any one particular gear—is overcome in order to make a shift. During a downshift, the same series of events occurs. The difference is that the power flow starts at the output shaft. Since power flow switches, the synchro rings use the opposite side of the teeth on a downshift. Sometimes a bad synchro will work on an upshift but grind on a downshift because the ring uses different aspects of itself.

One common misconception is that synchro rings cause jumping out of gear. In reality, synchros prevent grinding in gear. Therefore, if you make a clean shift and cannot keep the transmission in gear, you usually have worn "hard parts," such as a gear, shift fork, or slider. It can be one item or a combination of any of them.

The tiny clutch teeth transmit the power. If they get worn or twisted from lugging a transmission, the spline of the slider applies uneven pressure on the worn tooth and allows the two parts to slip away. A worn shift fork may not allow the slider and gear to engage fully, and a worn fork groove causes that same problem.

In the downshift mode, the slider is powered. In order for the slider to mate with the gear, it must index behind the gear. Whether you are upshifting or downshifting, a "block-out" condition can occur in which wear of the synchro assembly allows the ring and slider to meet point-to-point. The arrow shows the direction the ring must take in order for the slider to continue on its path to locking on the gear.

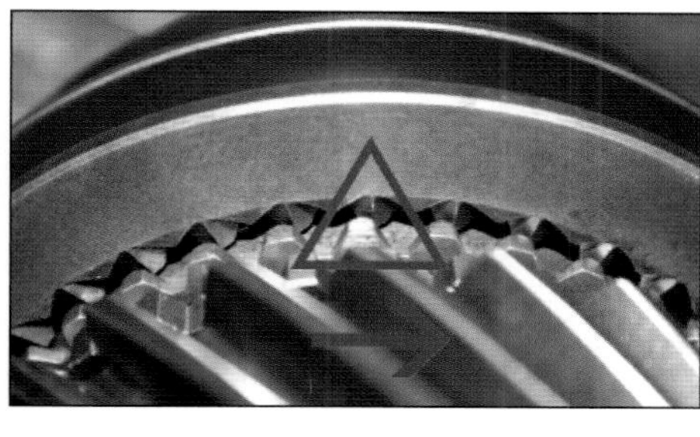

In the upshift mode, the gear is powered. In order for the slider to mate with the gear it must index ahead of the gear.

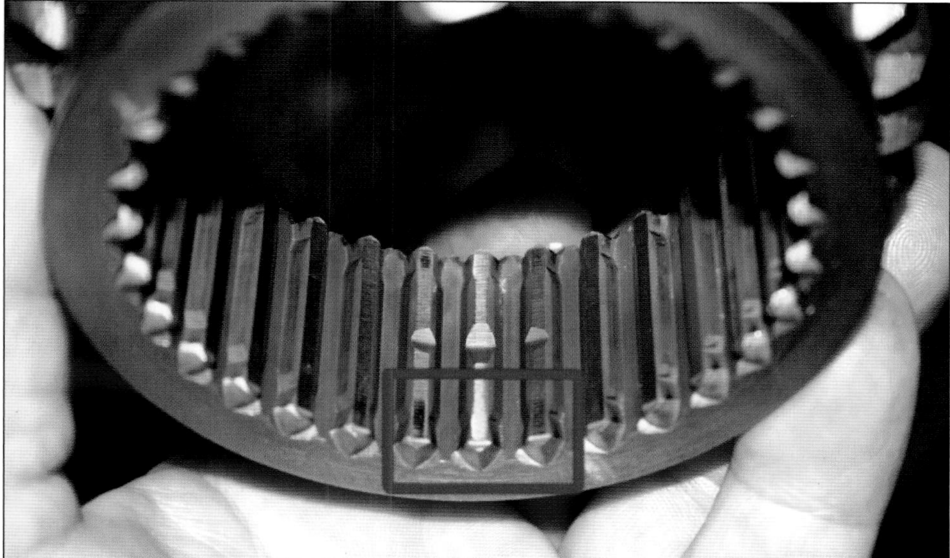

The back cut is referred to as a torque-locking spline, which forces the gear to stay engaged.

Torque locking sliders have the ends of their splines back cut. This, in effect, causes the clutch tooth of the gear to sort of fit in a pocket within the slider's spline, or it forces the gear to ramp in toward the center of the slider, whether you're on or off the gas. This design is common in most new transmissions. Some aftermarket gears for older transmissions are adding these features as well.

A synchro ring is nothing more than a cone clutch. The ring has a tapered inside diameter, which sits on a tapered cone of the gear. The ring has tiny threads, which lock onto the cone of the gear. In order for the ring to grab the gear properly, the ring's inside diameter has to be concentric with the mating surface of the gear, and it also has to be smaller. A good ring won't wobble or sit low on the gear. When a transmission grinds going into gear, the synchro ring has lost its ability to stop the gear. The ring is either warped or worn so much that no interference fit is left. I stress this issue because synchro rings are often blamed for jumping-out-of-gear problems or block-out problems.

Gear Design Basics

Today's transmission gears are computer designed to yield the maximum capacity in the smallest package. Fuel efficiency and preventing frictional losses are paramount. Often, people insist on purchasing NOS (new old stock) gears from the 1960s rather than new products offered by current aftermarket vendors. When it comes to old transmission gears, some people can't comprehend that in 40 years better methods of manufacturing have developed. The gearsets today can be made with more finely pitched helix angles to reduce noise. In addition, exotic alloys and profiles, which were next to impossible to mass-produce in the 1960s, are now being produced. Heat treating has also reached new levels of accuracy and control.

Early spur-gear designs were very strong but noisy and inefficient. Most 3- and 4-speed transmissions of the muscle car era used helical gears for quiet, efficient operation. General Motors' M22 Muncie 4-speed was the first semi-helical gearbox offered in a passenger car. The gears were at half the normal helix angle, creating a stronger but noisier transmission. This gear noise earned it the "Rockcrusher" nickname. Helical gears, because of their climbing nature, produce more heat and thrust loads. A spur-gear transmission hardly produces any thrust loads. Most transmissions destined for endurance racing use spur-gear designs because less heat is generated and little thrust loads are put on the bearings.

A synchro ring that sits correctly on the cone of the gear usually has a clearance of 0.050 inch.

The same bearing different raceways designed for 5/16- and 1/4-inch-diameter balls. The bearing that accepts the larger ball has a higher load rating.

When BorgWarner released the T5 5-speed in 1982, die-hard manual-shift enthusiasts laughed at the whole design. The T5 was the first American transmission that was truly computer designed. It was never intended for drag racing or road racing. It sported a smaller center-to-center distance than older muscle car 4-speeds and was designed for light- to medium-duty use. Now, nearly 30 years later, the OEM is still using it, and countless applications have been developed based on that radical design. This transmission started to change people's perception of transmission design, especially when it came to bearings.

Bearing Selection

Some form of a bearing supports upper and lower geartrains in any transmission design. The obvious reason for bearing use is to reduce friction. A properly selected bearing for an application withstands several different loads. The amount of thrust load, radial load, and RPM required for a particular application demands a certain style of bearing design. Helical gears produce both thrust and radial loads. Tapered bearings as well as ball bearings can handle both of these loads simultaneously. That is why they are frequently used in transmissions. Needle bearings are often found supporting countergears, but they cannot handle any thrust loading. That is why countergears employ the use of thrust washers.

Space can be a deciding factor for bearing selection as well. Tapered bearings (often called cup-and-cone bearings) can handle the same loads as a ball bearing but in a smaller format. Since tapered bearings are of a two-piece design, they require a preload or some means of keeping the cup and cone together. This is accomplished using a design that requires shims to set the preload. Usually a transmission that strictly uses tapered bearings is more expensive to produce than one using ball bearings.

There are always gains followed by losses when choosing a bearing. A big bearing may be able to handle a certain capacity issue, but the larger size may require a bigger case or longer center-to-center distance. There has been a debate about whether you can increase the capacity of a ball bearing by fitting the maximum allowable number of balls into the raceways. You can, up to a point. A standard ball bearing is called a "Conrad"-style bearing, and the bearing with the maximum number of balls is called a "Max Capacity" or "Filling Slot" bearing. Conrad-style bearings can have high raceway walls allowing for high-thrust capacities. The filling-slot bearing literally has slots in both the outer and inner raceways. The maximum number of balls can be dropped in the slots before the bearing cage is riveted into place. The problem is that the filling slot

A reduction in rated thrust capacity decreases the thrust loading of the bearing, which is not desirable when used with helical-cut gears because the drive angle of the gears naturally produces a thrust load. The filling-slot-style bearing is not recommended to use with helical gears.

Excessive heat in a filling-slot bearing caused the bearing cage to spread a drop on the inner raceway. Sometimes when bearings have too tight of fit tolerance heat will destroy them. To avoid this problem, I don't recommend using max-capacity bearing. Instead, stick to bearings that have a C3 fit rating.

reduces thrust capacity because the raceway walls now have an opening or may not be as high as a Conrad-style. However, this added number of balls increases radial load or up-and-down load.

Bearing design and ball size present some trade-offs as well. If you have a fixed diameter, you can fit more 1/4-inch-diameter balls than 5/16-inch-diameter balls in the same complement. One bearing may handle loads in one direction better than the other, and one may have more stability than the other. Ball bearings designed for industrial applications may have tighter clearances than the same-size bearing used in automotive applications. General automotive grade bearings have what is called a C3 fit. This looser fit enables dirt to pass through the raceways better. Part numbers of bearings are usually etched on the raceways.

All race and street transmissions I build use regular Conrad bearings. Max-capacity bearings develop more heat, which also kills the bearing's life. I've actually seen more failures with max-capacity bearings and generally avoid using them. The fact that a Conrad bearing is less expensive is an added bonus.

By the early 1980s we saw a trend in which transmission manufacturers placed needle bearings under each individual speed gear. Before that, gears rode directly on the shafts, with oil grooves or machined valleys for oil to gather in. It was an inexpensive process that made assembly very easy. Another alternative was sintered iron or bronze bushings. Almost all of the transmissions produced today use needle bearings under all the gears. This produces less drag (peristaltic drag) and allows the transmissions to shift easier. It also aids in achieving better fuel economy. Use of needle bearings under individual gears also prevents seizures at high speeds. Some early T10 and Muncie 4-speeds had rollerized first-speed gears. When used in endurance race situations, the first gear would get hot and weld itself to the mainshaft. Since first gear can be spinning more than two times faster than the output shaft it rides on, a car running at 7,000 rpm can come to a pretty nasty stop if first gear overheats.

When I think about the huge number of changes in the past few years in manufacturing, one thing sticks in my head. Advances in machine design and gear design software are allowing more and more people to create stronger, more efficient and easier-to-shift transmissions. The world is truly a better place to shift in.

Transmission Assembly Tips and Techniques

The transmissions outlined in this book were chosen because of their popularity as well as their capacity to be rebuilt with common shop tools. Although you may want to rebuild a transmission not outlined in this book, you must realize that the cost of certain specialty tools required for a one-time job may not be justified. Please take the time to read all of the build-ups. Some of the tips and techniques used on one transmission may be used on another as well, or on one not covered in this book. Investing in factory shop manuals is a great ideaIt's important to comprehend why the specialty tools are needed and what their function is. Working on a transmission you have never worked on before without any form of reference is a recipe for disaster. You may find that a required tool's function may be duplicated by another means that you have at your disposal. I remember a Doug Nash overdrive having needed a special spring compressor and retaining-bolt kit. A shop press and three standard 8-mm bolts served the same function.

Typical kits sell for under $200 and make a rebuild quite easy. Be aware that all kits are not alike, and kit parts have a great range of quality from very high to poor. It is best to ask what components come with the kit before making a purchase. (See "Choosing a Premium Rebuild Kit" on page 32.) Better companies offer support.

Professional Mechanic Tip

PRO TIP

Aluminum bar stock, old bearing races, used wrist pins, or the other pieces you see here are useful during a transmission rebuild.

So What Do I Use?

Manual transmissions can be quite old, so if you are going to do a rebuild and not a quick repair, I suggest you purchase a rebuild kit. These kits include all wearable parts, such as bearings, synchro rings, thrust washers, needle bearings, gaskets, and seals. High-grade kits have OEM bearings and gaskets. Less expensive kits may have "no name" bearings, which are not worth the $30 savings.

As far as tools go, a basic tool kit is a good starting point. Tools that have a lifetime warranty form a basic foundation and are a wise investment. Hydraulic shop presses can be purchased for under $200. They are great for gear work and prove useful for other projects as well. A few different-size bearing clamps, old transmission cases, piston wrist pins, aluminum round stock, and bearing races are great additions to your collection of press tools.

An assortment of snap-ring and retaining-ring pliers is always needed. I've purchased pliers at swap meets at rock-bottom prices. Buy up cheap retaining-ring pliers so that you can grind them if needed for specialty work. Old driveshaft yokes help you align tailhousings, and make sure the rear bushings are installed correctly. These also help you spin a transmission. Pry bar sets and screwdrivers, which you don't mind using for anything but screws, are ideal for this work. Two-jaw or three-jaw pullers are nice, but I rarely use them. Propane torches for heating parts help install slip-on components, such as steel speedo gears that could get ruined by pressing or hammering them in place. Telescopic magnets are great for removing detent balls. Cheap dental-tool kits are great for removing O-rings and retrieving detent springs. I prefer nonserrated steak knives for removing gaskets rather than special gasket "scrapers." Copper scouring pads are great for removing silicone sealant without marring aluminum surfaces. A big mistake is to use an air-powered rotary scouring pad to remove gaskets. This ruins the precision flat surface of the case and will lead to leaks.

A vise holds some transmissions, but building a custom holding fixture is the way to go if you plan on doing volume work. Personally, I've never used a holding fixture because setting up a transmission fixture is a time-consuming process. By following the techniques detailed in this book, a fixture simply isn't required.

If you are going to clean your own parts, then you should invest in the proper cleaning tank, safety glasses, and gloves. It is easier just to send all of your parts to a production

Be creative! I find cheap party platters at the Dollar Store and use them as parts organizers.

Copper scouring pads are abrasive enough to easily remove sealant.

Special Tool

Special chisels used for muffler work make removing tailhousing bushings a snap.

Insert the cutting edge of the chisel along the oil-feed passage and tap out the bushing.

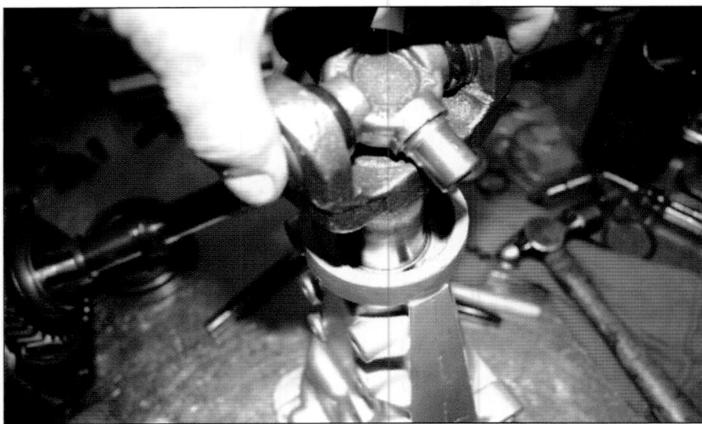

Use an old driveshaft yoke to make sure your new bushing is pressed in properly.

Professional Mechanic Tip

Dremel rotary tools have a reinforced cut-off wheel, which makes for very easy deburring. Reinforced wheels do not shatter and are much safer to use. I prefer 1- to 1½-inch wheels using a 1/8-inch mandrel. I save all the discs that wear to smaller diameters for work in tight places.

This front countershaft bore has been bushed to restore its center-to-center distance. It also creates a larger steel surface area and tighter press fit, and it prevents leaks. For performance applications, rebushing both front and rear bores and moving the countergear up a few thousands of an inch helps reduce gear deflection.

transmission shop and pay to have them pressure cleaned.

I also don't have air in my shop. Instead, I use electric impact guns. I hate the noise of compressors, and I don't like blowing off parts because it creates more airborne contaminants. You can get small air compressors for under $300 that even come with starter air tool kits. In addition, a small can of compressed air typically used for cleaning computers is usually adequate for the one-time job.

If you are rebuilding a transmission and you require the installation of new gears, you may need to deburr them. A Dremel rotary tool with cut-off wheel is ideal for cleaning up gears.

Bench grinders, drill presses, and a 4-inch disc grinder should be acquired for more serious work, such as slick-shifting gears or clearancing gears by cutting them back a bit.

Repairing Castings

A transmission doesn't have to fail to have its fair share of problems. The environment and service people can be a hazard as well. I've seen people run over objects, drop transmissions, and get into accidents. This leads to cracks, holes, and stripped threads.

Aluminum and cast-iron cases can be heli-arc welded. Welding broken mounting ears, caused by people pulling a transmission into the engine with bolts, is a common job, which should be done by a professional. You can warp a transmission case easily by using too much heat. Epoxies, such as J-B Weld, are great for fixing small cracks or porosity problems. Drilling and tapping out a small hole and then plugging it with a bolt is also an alternative to welding.

Alloy main cases tend to stretch when a gearset explodes. Muncie and T10 transmissions have a tendency to leak from the front countershaft bore.

Gear Preparation

Inspect gears for typical cracks, chips, and obvious missing teeth. Gears with missing teeth do not work. Since the gears in most manual-shift transmissions are in constant mesh, if the teeth are broken on one gear, usually the matching gear exhibits some form of damage or stress caused by the upper gear slamming against it. Often, people ask to purchase a new input shaft because the old one is missing three teeth. I ask them if they want to purchase a new matching countergear, and the response is usually "no," because that gear is not missing any teeth. These people haven't noticed the bent, cracked, or deformed teeth. As a rule, if one gear has broken teeth, always change the matching gear, too. When transmissions are run low on oil, gears can become blue or black in color. Usually the front gears starve of oil because oil moves to the back of the transmission when a car accelerates. Gears appear scuffed looking or gouged out in the center of the tooth. Chipped teeth are another story.

Debris getting lodged in the gear usually causes chipping in gears. Sliding gears that are non-synchronized, such as most reverse gears, also have chips. Some gears are simply chipped by poor assembly or handling techniques. It's quite common for many new gears in boxes to have their share of dings and chips. Any transmissions I build also have the gears completely deburred. You can deburr most chipped gears just as long as the chipped section is no longer than one-quarter the length of the gear tooth and never extends into the root or center section of the gear tooth.

Anti-rattle or anti-backlash plates are quite common in Muncie, Chrysler, and Saginaw transmissions. These spring-loaded plates are offset in relationship to the actual tooth profile. I cut these plates off because they can loosen up in a performance application.

Bolts and Threads

Older transmissions may have bolts that are seized in place. Using an impact gun is a sure way to either strip or snap the bolt. If a bolt seems hard to remove, try heating it first with a propane torch and strike it with a hammer. You want to hit the bolt flat on the head. The idea is to stretch the threads enough to loosen the bolt. Hex-socket pipe plugs easily strip. To remove really difficult bolts, heat and strike them, and then use a hammer to drive a Torx bit into the hex bore. Slamming the Torx bit into the plug deforms the threads and produces a stronger contact pattern to make a stripped hex plug removable.

1 Inspect Gears

The gear on the left has heavily worn engagement teeth, which hold the transmission "in gear." It is worn to such a degree that it will disengage or fall out of gear. In comparison, the new gear on the right shows how much material is actually missing from the gear on the left.

Important!

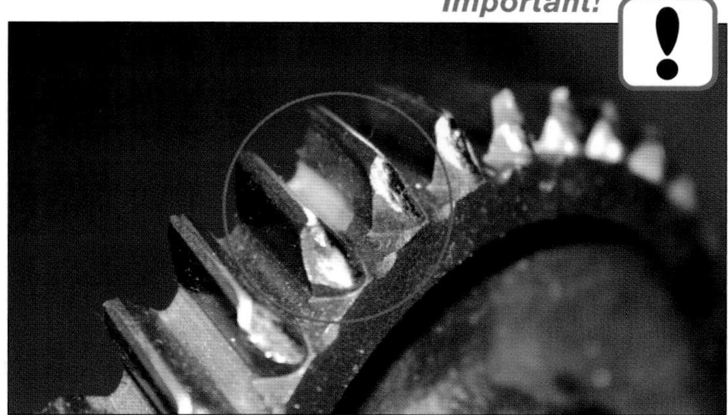

This is common damage on a Muncie reverse gear. The gear is still usable because both chipped ends overhang each other when engaged. This damage is always evident in gears that are unsynchronized and the overhang design is built into them.

2 Repair Damaged Threads

Fastener threads strip out from time to time, but they are easy enough to repair. Inserts designed to repair threads, such as those made by Heli-Coil, have special taps and drill sizes. Only use the recommended drill and tap.

The insertion tool winds the drive tang into place. Once it's seated, the drive tang is snapped off.

The threaded inserts form standard-size threads from nonstandard threads. Tool supply companies and most auto parts stores usually have these readily available.

Before removing the drive tang, check to see that the new thread actually works. You can use needle-nose pliers to grasp the tang and pull out the insert if your installation doesn't work.

If a bolt has broken off, try to get the remaining surface as flat as possible. Use a sharp centering punch in the middle of the bolt. The centering punch helps you start a drill. Drill with a small bit first and work up to the size of the bore so that you can install a threaded insert.

When you have stripped threads, the wrong thing to do is rethread to a larger size. That is unprofessional. Threaded inserts from Heli-Coil make it possible to restore damaged threads to the correct size. The hole is tapped using a special tap that allows a threaded insert to be screwed into the bore. Once the insert is installed, the drive tang is broken off and the thread is restored.

Hydraulic Press Basics

There is one basic rule when using a press. That is to only press and support the part against the area that is holding the press fit. For example, if a bearing is held in a housing by the outer race, press against that outer race. If the bearing is held on by the inner race, press or support against that inner race. If you support against the inner race and press against the outer race, you will deform the raceways, and basically damage the part. I cut apart older bearings and use the old races as support surfaces. I've purchased cheap socket sets and use the sockets

3 Load Needles in Countergear

The first step is to place the spacer tube in the countergear. Be sure to use plenty of grease.

A generous amount of grease provides ample adhesion, so you can load the needles into place.

Once everything is in place, push the countershaft you are going to use through the gear, but hold a thrust washer in the front to prevent parts coming out of the opposite end.

Inspect the countergear to ensure you've added as many needles as possible and they are all in place.

as press tools as well. However, never hammer on hardened parts.

Loading Needle Bearings

People seem to have a hard time loading needle bearings in countergears. The thought of loading more than 100 bearings in a gear can be intimidating. Oddly, most factory shop manuals advocate the use of "dummy shafts," to load needles. I always say, "Dummy shafts are for dummies." The problem with the dummy shaft is that you don't see the needles or the position of the needles in the gear. You can't see if you've put in the proper number of needles. When removing the dummy shaft and sliding in the real shaft in place, sometimes the needles can drop, which means starting over again.

Consider the following procedure and the thought process behind it. I use grease to pack the needles in place. You can use wheel-bearing grease if the transmission is using conventional 75W-90 gear lubes. There are new assembly lubes, such as Trans Gel and Trans Goo. These assembly gels break down faster for both gear lube and automatic transmission fluid applications. They also seem to retain viscosity better in colder or warmer climates. If you're working in a 96-degree shop in Florida, wheel-bearing grease will not hold as well as an assembly gel.

4 Inspect Syncro Ring

Critical Inspection

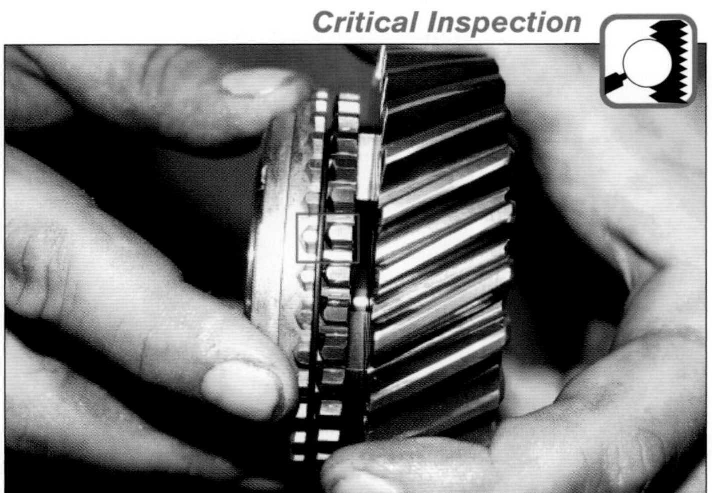

Synchro rings should be fitted and checked on each gear. Don't assume that a new ring is okay. I've seen many rings with defective machining or warping—you can warp a new ring by simply dropping it on the floor. A good ring should not wobble on the gear cone. It should fit firmly and lock to the gear while applying pressure to the ring as you rotate the gear. Make sure the ring is not sitting too high or too low. The average ring gap is 0.030 to 0.060 inch. A low-fitting ring makes for poor lock up and displaced strut keys. A high-fitting ring can cause binding. A worn gear cone that shows defined ridges prevents a ring from properly grabbing the gear. Sometimes a ring may lock well on one gear but not another. You can also use lapping compound, which is basically an abrasive paste to fit a ring to a gear. Once rings are fitted, the "set" is put aside until the build begins. Always fit rings, and never just place new rings on gears.

This ring looks good. However, if you look at the backside of the ring it sits too low and hits the gear. Therefore, this ring needs to be replaced.

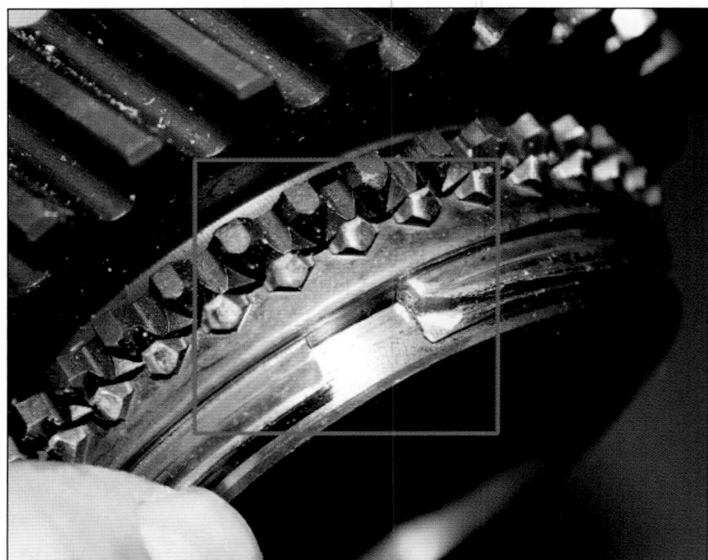

When a ring has ballooned and sits too low, it cannot lock on the gear cone, which causes grinding when in gear. As the ring moves away from the strut key, the additional gap allows the strut keys to pop out and further damage the ring. You can see how slipping struts have damaged the key slot.

Here are typically worn teeth on a slider. Once the teeth lose their point definition, they can ruin synchro rings and gears if not replaced because the teeth do not effectively mesh.

This is a 3-4 slider for a Muncie 4-speed. Installing it in the 1-2 position will cause the edge to hit the lower counter gear. Notice that this edge is square. It's important to recognize these subtle differences.

This slider's edge has a taper, which means it will clear the lower gear when the slider is engaged.

5 Inspect Spline Taper

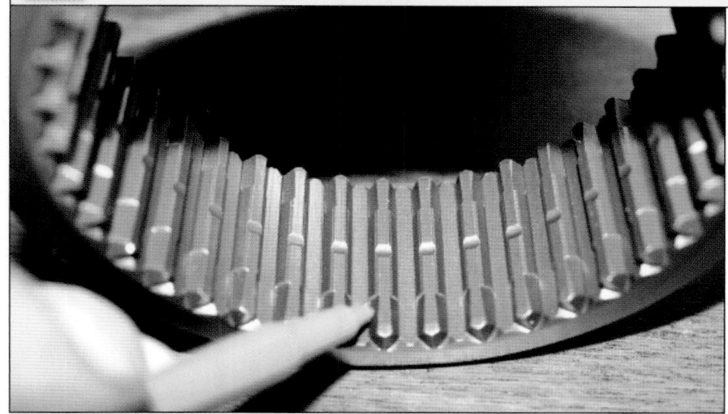

This taper is purposely machined into the spline. The back taper or "torque-locking" design forces the gear's engagement teeth to ramp toward the center, so it doesn't fall out of gear.

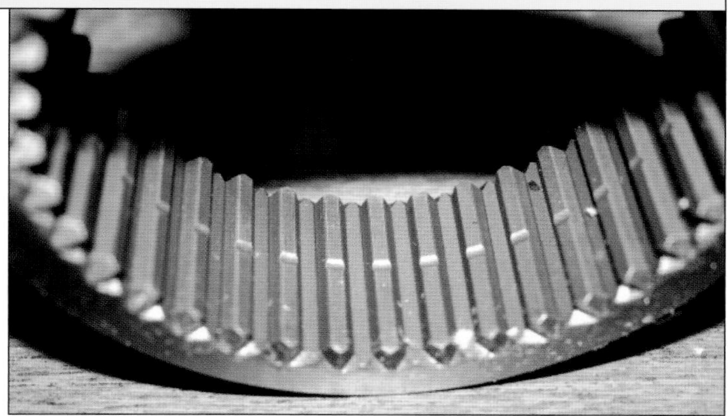

Here is a standard-design internal slider spline. It should be used if the matching gears are in pristine condition. If the transmission tends to fall out of gear, the torque-locking sliders are better suited.

Critical Inspection

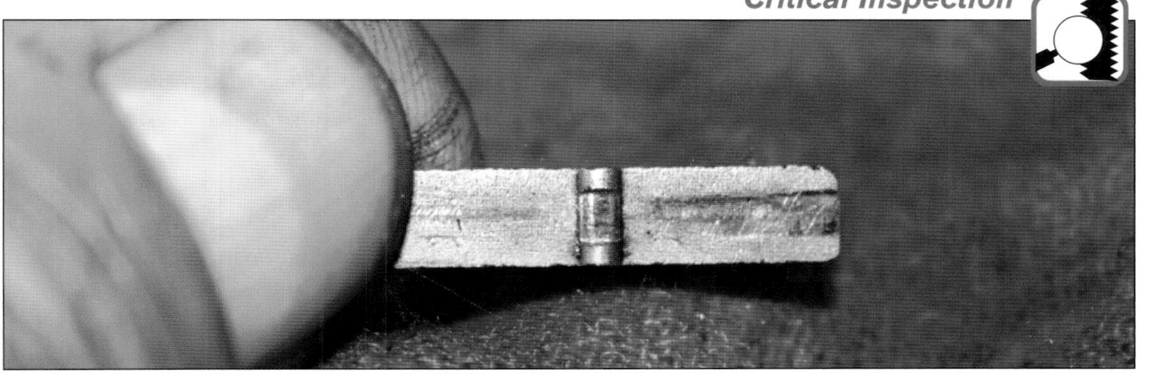

Always check the strut keys for wear. If the keys show significant wear, they should be replaced. This key has been worn flat and definitely needs to be replaced.

6 Assemble Synchro Gears and Parts

Important!

Start by placing the slider within the hub and make sure the slider's notches line up with the key slots. Some sliders have notches on all the splines; others have them in just in three places. It's a good idea to use a felt-tip marker to indicate where the notches are. If the notches are not lined up correctly with the synchro strut key slots in the hub, the synchro will not work.

Place all of the struts or dogs in their hub slots.

When using a hollow key, the spring tang usually is placed in the center of the key. Otherwise, it is alongside it. Insert the spring in a clockwise direction.

Flip the synchro assembly over and install the second spring in a clockwise direction. When assembled, the springs will be opposite of one another and create a nice balance.

This completed assembly shows solid-design strut keys. I usually grind the spring tangs, so they don't hit the inside wall of the hub. This helps to provide a clean, positive shift.

When loading the needles you can only load as many as will fit. There is no need to count. If you can fit one more needle, then you need that extra needle. Once I have all of my needles loaded, I take the counter-shaft I'm going to use and push it through the gear. I hold a thrust washer on the opposite end of the gear to keep all the needles from getting pushed out, and then I push the shaft through. This adds some extra packing and squeezes out extra grease. I rotate the shaft in the gear because this allows me to check for binding and smooth rotation. Next, I then remove the shaft, which allows me to inspect the needles and check for complete rows, good alignment, and proper spacing. A dummy shaft cannot be used for any of these checks because the gear has been installed in the case after the shaft is removed.

7 Remove Bearing

If the bearing locates from the outside diameter, press or tap it in place from the outside of the case.

If the bearing locates from the inside diameter, press or tap it in place from the inside race. Its best to use a press, but a punch will work if the fit is a slip or snug fit.

Precision Measurement

8 Check Snap-Ring Clearance

It's simple to check snap-ring clearance. First, verify that the edge of the ring fits the groove before installing it. Then use a micrometer to measure the width of the groove and thickness of the ring. Dialing-in the correct endplay is a matter of subtracting the width of the groove from the thickness of the ring.

Subassemblies and Synchronizers

Some of the basic assembly techniques pictured in this section are used in just about every build listed in this book. Rather than repeat these steps with each build, they are shown here only.

The synchro slider can exhibit wear on the teeth, but can also have an enlarged groove for the shift fork. Common causes for falling out of gear are worn engagement teeth on the slider and gear combined with a worn shift-fork groove and worn shift fork.

Strut keys or shift dogs always give people assembly problems because they are spring loaded. Rather than assemble in this order: springs, keys, and slider, which is how most shop manuals tell you how to do it, simply place the slider on the hub first, then the keys and then the springs.

This is a modular approach of fitting synchro rings to the gears and creating component subassemblies aids in building a quality transmission. They offer the rebuilder a simple way to perform quality checks. If you have more than one person working in a shop, it is a good idea to have your subassemblies inspected by someone else and vise-versa. Sometimes another set of eyes is all that is needed to prevent a potential disaster.

Bearing Tips

Misdiagnosing bearing noise usually leads to a worthless rebuild. The majority of people cannot distinguish between bearing noise and gear noise. Once bearings develop

9 Verify Bearing Dimensions and Condition

Here is a typical sealed bearing. New designs always use them. This bearing had more than 100,000 miles and when I pulled the seals the bearing still looked pretty good. Most manufacturers today are using bearings made in the United States or Japan. If you need to replace the bearing, always use the OEM replacement bearing. Sometimes getting a bearing from a bearing supply house is not really a good idea because automotive-grade bearings require different fits and tapers.

I've taken the sealed bearing apart. If you look carefully you can see how one side of the bearing has more wear than the other due to the nature of thrust loads from the helical-cut gears.

BONUS CONTENT:
Scan to learn about the basics of ball bearings, needle bearings, and tapered bearings.

Important!

Not all bearings of the same dimension are alike. This is something you must detect. The new bearing on the left has a slight chamfer to the inside diameter (ID). The ID of the older inner raceway has a very square cut bore with no chamfer. The bore with no chamfer is a better thrust surface and will support a snap ring better. Better designs use a spacer in front of the raceway to maximize snap-ring holding capacity.

imperfections in the raceways and balls, these imperfections generate noise and vibration. Dust and debris in a bearing can cause noise when spinning it by hand, especially after cleaning a bearing in solvent that has debris in it! Try to get a light into the bearing to inspect the raceways for pits or craters. These usually appear as dark pits.

A bad bearing produces sort of a growling, erratic noise because the components of the bearing never hit the exact same spot by the next revolution. However, gear noise is never erratic; it's consistent. A broken tooth may translate into a knocking noise that gets faster as the RPM goes up. A whine or hum may change pitch with engine RPM, suggesting worn or mismatched gears.

In 4-speed operation, in which fourth gear is a direct drive, the input and output shafts are locked and reduce loads on the bearings and gears. This can cause the noise of bad gears or bearings to diminish when in fourth gear. Bearings are relatively cheap. There is no point in reusing 40-year-old bearings when the new bearings of today exhibit better quality standards.

Sometimes transmissions have selective snap rings to set endplay. Often the tightest fitting ring works, since gear clearances for oil are usually built into the design. Some early T10 4-speeds actually lock up with a snap ring that is too thick.

If I can find an equivalent bearing with seals for an application, I will use it. Dirt is the main cause of bearing failure; seals keep the dirt out. Oil actually still gets past the seals and keeps it lubricated.

Gaskets and Sealants

Good-quality gaskets save you a great deal of headaches. Try to use original-equipment gaskets when possible. There are several companies that now reproduce gaskets

10 Use Gaskets and Sealants

Anaerobic sealants, such as #51813 from Permatex, seal on contact. These are currently used in a great many of OEM applications. I coat gasket surfaces with this sealant or use it in applications that do not require gaskets.

I always coat both sides of the case so the gasket is between a skin coat of sealant. It makes for easy removal of the gasket and cleanup.

Grease the internal lip of the seal and spring.

11 Drive Seal into Tailhousing

You can use a hammer or plastic mallet to drive a seal in place just as long as you do it carefully and avoid distorting the seal. Also coat the outer shell of the seal with sealant, which prevents oil from leaking around the seal due to surface imperfections.

12 Wipe Off Sealant from Housing

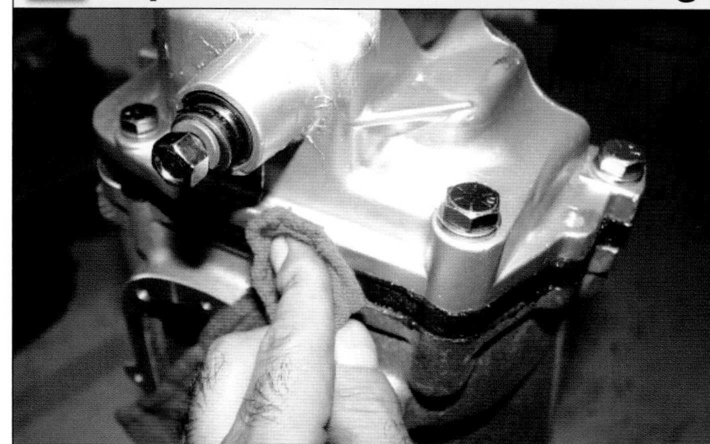

Taking the time to wipe off excess sealant makes a better-looking rebuild and shows that you are a professional.

using the same compounds the factory did years ago. I always coat both gasket surfaces with either RTV Silicone or anaerobic sealant. I prefer the anaerobic because it sets on contact and cures within 20 minutes. This is great if you need to get something sealed up quickly and back in the car. Silicone sealants don't cure that fast. If a transmission requires a gasket, use one.

Using gasket eliminators may be great for an oil pan or valve cover, but sometimes the gaskets in manual transmissions actually set the spacing of the gears as well as endplay. Certain front-bearing retainers crack when using sealant only, because the gasket fills the gap between the two parts. Without the gasket, you might bend the retainer around the bearing and crack it as you tighten the bolts.

Most lip seals have an outer steel shell with the rubber seal vulcanized onto it. A circular spring surrounds the inside diameter of the seal to maintain its shape as well as contact with the shaft. Before installing any lip seal, grease the seal. Applying a liberal coating of grease to the seal aids in initial lubrication of the seal as well as using the grease to hold the spring in place.

Certain case castings have bolt holes that break into the inside. Most front bearing retainers have bolts that go right into the case. Oil can leak past the threads, so it is important to use some sort of sealant in these areas.

Taking the time to wipe off excess sealant makes for a better looking rebuild, and shows that you are a professional.

Choosing a Premium Rebuild Kit

Manual-transmission rebuild kits were rarely available to the general public 30 years ago. Parts were usually obtained through car dealers and parts stores only. The lack of availability of parts forced me to either build or find companies that made the parts for the OEMs. In 1981 I started to sell my own designed kits to the public at car shows each year. I made 12 different kits for popular transmissions. (I define a rebuild kit as a kit that replaces all wearable components in a transmission, except for "hard parts." These "wearables" are bearings, synchro rings, gaskets, seals, strut keys, bushings, a countershaft, and small parts, such as needle bearings, snap rings, slingers, thrust washers, and various clips and springs.)

A good kit is well thought out and includes everything you need, plus a few extras. Today, unfortunately, companies that don't rebuild transmissions themselves are selling kits, or sales people who don't know what should or should not be in a kit are selling them. An example is the Muncie 4-speed kits, which are now made by many manufacturers.

A high-quality kit starts with high-quality bearings made in the United States or Japan. Kits having bearings with no name or country of origin on them should not be used. Synchro rings, which are original equipment, should be used whenever possible. The aftermarket T5 cast-brass rings I've seen have only a fraction of the strength of the factory-forged bronze alloy rings. (Always ask if the rings are forged or cast.) Cheap kits usually lack a countershaft, which more than likely will need to be replaced since it is a bearing surface. Good kits include tail bushings, strut keys, front nuts, and slingers. These are all important items that you will need and are usually left out of cheaper kits.

I have found differences in the fit of front nuts in Muncie kits. Try to get kits with American-made nuts or check the fit. Loose thread causes the nut to loosen in operation. Good gaskets usually have a manufacturer name on the paper they are stamped from. No-name gaskets fall into the same category as no-name bearings and should be avoided. A high-quality kit has bronze or Babbitt-backed thrust washers, just like the OEM. Cheap kits often contain replacement washers made out of stamped steel that will cause premature wear on your gear's thrust surfaces.

I have seen insignificant things added to kits to make them more attractive in lieu of quality parts, such as tubes of sealant or cans of paint. Sometimes the kits are padded with cheap sliders or shift forks to appear more equipped, but these still lack quality components. When you do make a purchase, be sure you are able to get quality support if you need it. That is the most important consideration.

BorgWarner Transmissions

BorgWarner was one of the largest manufacturers of manual-shift transmissions in the United States. Ford and General Motors primarily made their own manual transmissions from the 1950s to the 1970s. Chrysler Transmission Development evolved into a company called New Process Gear. The majority of its transmissions were used in Chrysler products, but years later, that company was sold to competitors as well.

From left to right: Chrysler A833, ST10, and Muncie countergears. The A833 is longer because it incorporates the reverse idler as part of the gear. And of course, the A833 provides exceptional strength.

BorgWarner was different because it had no affiliation with any automobile manufacturer. The company sold its designs to any manufacturer as well as directly to the public via auto parts stores. It also made replacement parts for everyone's transmissions, something only a few companies ever succeeded at. Companies, such as Republic Gear and Perfection Hy-Test, did the same thing, but oddly, today none of these companies produce any gears. This is important because you can find variations of certain BorgWarner transmissions in many makes and models.

T10 4-Speed History and Facts

BorgWarner produced many 3-speeds, such as the T85, T86, T87, T14, T15, and the T16. The first passenger-car 4-speed was the T10. In fact, it was the first American passenger-car 4-speed! It was based on the T85 design. Some T10 part numbers today still use the T85 prefix.

The T10 became an option in Corvettes in May 1957. Keep in mind that power levels of engines

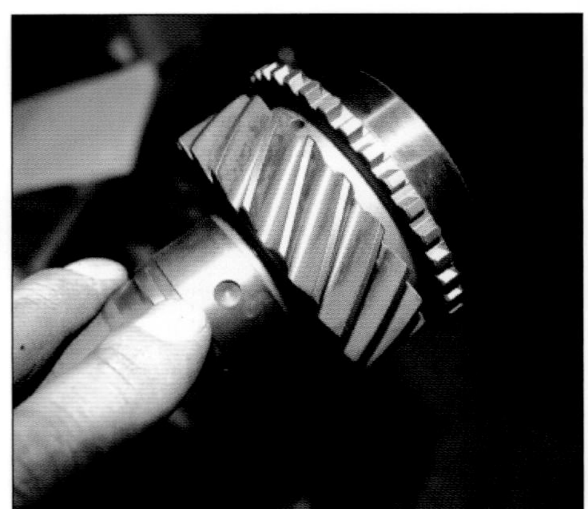

The 9310 Nickel T10 gears can be identified by drill marks on the shaft. 9310 was a high-performance alloy used from the 1960s to the 1980s. Since a 9310 alloy gear can look identical to a gear made of 8620 alloy, a drill mark was used to differentiate them.

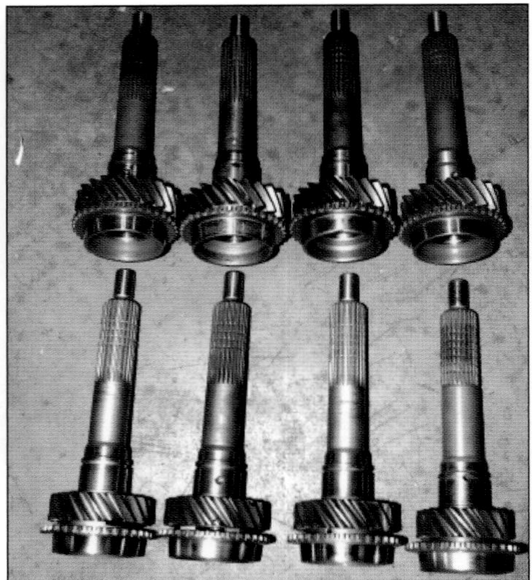

Super T10 GM Input Shafts. Note the various identification grooves and drill marks. The grooves identify the transmission ratio, and the drill mark indicates it is a 9310 alloy.

were climbing, and as a result, the T10 design had to change as well. Gears became wider, and alloys were changed. Unfortunately, there wasn't an emphasis on documenting changes. For example, early third-speed gears have a bronze bushing and matching-diameter mainshaft, which do not interchange with later gears and shafts, but in GM versions only.

Early T10 transmissions were used in General Motors and Ford Products. As horsepower levels increased, GM designed the Muncie and Ford designed the Toploader. GM replaced the T10 with the Muncie in mid 1963. Ford kept both the T10 and Toploader in production at the same time. Certain optioned cars received a Toploader while others a T10. I still haven't come across specific data that says which Ford cars got which transmission.

To accommodate increasing power levels, BorgWarner designed the Super T10. This transmission featured gears with a wide cut and a coarse pitch for better capacity. It eliminated a thrust bearing between second and third gear to tighten up on endplay issues and ditched alloy main cases in favor of nodular iron cases, which yielded a 50 percent increase in tensile strength. Ford and AMC used these "First Design" Super T10 transmissions from 1965 to the early to mid 1970s. BorgWarner also implemented its Power Brute Parts line. This gave individuals the ability to purchase upgraded components, gears, and complete replacement transmissions from their local speed shop or auto parts store.

These aftermarket transmissions offered special gear ratios. Again, this made the T10 a favorite among drag racers because the ratios gave people certain performance advantages over their stock units. The Super T10 gear ratios were designed to improve acceleration. You could get an ST10 with a 2.42, 2.64, 2.88, and 3.44 first gear.

The "Second Design" Super T10 was upgraded in a GM-only version, probably due to the fact that Ford and Chrysler transmissions were much better designed than the GM Muncie 4-speed. In fact, it was quite common to adapt the Chrysler Hemi 4-speed to GM applications for drag-race use. The Second Design Super T10 added 26 splines to the input shaft and 32 splines to the output shaft to combat twisting. It increased the countershaft diameter from 7/8 to 1 inch, sleeved first gear (for improved oiling), used a cast-iron side cover to eliminate flex, and eliminated O-ring grooves on the forward shifter shafts to improve strength. The standard alloy ST10 was 8620, but the over-the-counter race units could be ordered with 9310 alloy gears for improved capacity.

The following is a quick reference guide for the ST10. Only first-gear ratios can be identified by the input-shaft ID grooves.

Gear	Ratio	Manufacturer
None	3.42	Pontiac
6	3.42	Chevrolet
5	2.88	GM
4	2.88	Aftermarket
3	2.64	All
2	2.43	All

A whole book could be written about T10 identification because many design changes occurred during production. In 1975, when horsepower levels dropped and gas mileage was a concern, GM replaced the Muncie with the ST10. The advantage was the ST10's better first-gear ratios. These worked with more economical axle ratios, such as a 3.08. These Super T10s should not be confused with the replacement over-the-counter transmissions. The ratios and lightweight cases were designed for their intended use, making them weaker than the Muncie 4-speed but better suited to the axle ratios.

The Super T10 was used in GM vehicles from 1975 to 1983 as a 4-speed. The 1982–1983 F-Body Camaro/Firebird had an oddball version with a passenger-mount shifter, to centralize the stick to make it compatible with the 5-speed option. Doug Nash Engineering made a 2.88:1 first-gear version coupled to an automatic overdrive for the 1984–1988 Corvette; it was the 4+3. From looking at casting numbers in about 1982, Doug Nash Engineering purchased the rights to the T10 name and design. The design flaws of several components led to seal failures and made the 4+3 a very problematic transmission.

By late 1987 Doug Nash Engineering closed and Richmond Gear purchased the rights to the ST10 and all of Doug Nash's designs. The buy-out made sense because Richmond Gear was making most of the gears anyway. Today, the GM replacement ST10 4-speed can be purchased new from Richmond Gear, making it the longest running production 4-speed.

BorgWarner Transmissions

Number	Transmission
10	T10 4-speed
294	New Process A833
296	Ford Toploader
297	Muncie 4-speed
301	Saginaw 3- and 4-speed
302	Saginaw 4-speed
307	New Process A833 (later style)

Part Type	Part Name
1	Main Case
2	Main Shaft
3	Countershaft
6	Front Bearing Retainer
7	Extension Housing
8	Countergear
12	1st Gear
21 & 31	2nd Gear
11	3rd Gear
16	Input Shaft
14	Synchro Ring
83	Synchro Ring
15	Synchro Sleeve
2.5	Synchro Hub
10	Reverse Idler Front and Rear
34	Reverse Idler Rear
23	Shift Fork
148	Side Cover
35	Reverse Idler Shafts
36 & 46	Mainshaft Reverse Gears
40 & 41	Selector Shafts
50	Small Parts Kits

This is your basic early T10. It has a nine-bolt side cover and no external shifter shaft seals. BorgWarner used the same basic design for GM, Ford, and AMC cars. This is a T-10 from a GM car.

Rebuilding T10 4-Speeds

Although the T10 and Super T10 may look the same, internal differences require slightly different disassembly procedures. The build techniques are similar to the Muncie, and after a while, one becomes proficient at building this style of transmission. Like the Muncie, they have a side cover, a mid-plate-supported mainshaft, reverse shifter shaft in the tailhousing and a countergear supported by a pressed-in countershaft with loose needle roller bearings and thrust washers. The mainshaft and all the gears can be pulled out of the T10 transmission while the countergear and input shaft remain in place. The Super T10 countergear must be dropped first, or the front bearing removed, in order for the upper geartrain to clear the countergear during removal.

BorgWarner Numbering System

With so much misinformation perpetuated by the Internet and online auctions, the BorgWarner numbering system can be your ace in the hole. The early system used a transmission model ID number followed by a part type, followed by a variation. T, AT, WT, or AWT was used on all of these ID numbers. The "A" could stand for Aftermarket, but this is used and mixed with standard factory numbers. The "T" more than likely means Transmission and "WT," Warner Transmission.

Here's how the early system worked. A countergear for a Ford Toploader is WT296-8. However, a WT296-8A is the same transmission but a different ratio gear. A Muncie 4-speed's first gear is a WT297-12. Since there are three variations of Muncie first-speed gears, there is a WT297-12, WT297-12A, and WT297-12B. There are other less significant part types, such as designators for seals and bushings, but these parts are now in modern rebuild kits.

Richmond Gear bought the T10, and Tremec Corporation purchased the T5 and T56. Tremec maintains BorgWarner's numbering system on existing production transmissions, including the T5 and T56. New units now have some different numbers that are just starting to evolve as of this writing. Tremec's own transmissions, such as the TKO series, have nothing to do with these systems.

Since 1970, Warner Gear used a 10-digit numbering system. Old parts that were unchanged kept the old numbers, but if they were revised or improved for any reason, a new 10-digit number was assigned. The first four digits represent the model transmission. The next three define the part category. The final three digits identify the version of that part. A typical number could be 13-52-080-030.

Transmission Model Designators–The First 4 Digits

Number	Transmission Type
10-00	Miscellaneous Standard Parts
13-00	Miscellaneous Standard Parts
13-04	T10 4-speed
13-32	SR4 4-speed (Ford)
13-38	T50 5-speed
13-40	SR4 4-speed (AMC)
13-50	Ford Ranger Transfer Case
13-51	T4 4-speed
13-52	T5 5-speed
13-53	T4C 4-speed
13-81	T45 5-speed
13-86	T56 6-speed

There are many truck, 3-speed, and transfer-case models that were left off this list. These numbers are also used in casting numbers on main cases, making it easy to identify the type of transmission.

Component Part Category–The Next 3 Digits

Number	Transmission Type
027	Bearing Caps and Retainers
031	Flanges and Yokes
037	Shims
039	Covers
065	Transmission Cases
066	Extension Housings
067	Intermediate Shafts, Torque Carrying
068	Intermediate Shafts, non Torque Carrying
070	Gears Splines or Keyed
077	Countergears
080	Gears, Free Running (1st, 2nd, 3rd, and 5th)
083	3rd Speed, Free Running
084	Idler Gears
085	Input Shafts
089	Synchro Sleeves
090	Synchro Hubs
091	Synchro Rings
096	Shift Forks and Lugs
097	Shift Covers
098	Shift Levers
100	Shift Rails
127	Bushings and Wear Pads
171	Mainshafts
671	Mainshaft Assemblies

The above example, 13-52-080-030, decodes as a T5 5-speed free-running gear. It's actually a first-speed gear, but unlike the early system, we cannot determine what kind of gear type it is by part number alone. (I've also left out small parts to focus on numbers that a person would actually come across.)

Because the system has been in use for decades, it is due for another change. Newer T5 5-speeds manufactured by Tremec now have TTET designators, such as the T45 5-speed–TNET, T56 6-speed–TNET or TUET, the TKO/3550 5-speed–TCET, and the new 3650–TDET.

T10 Disassembly

1 Remove Side Cover

Use a 1/2-inch socket and ratchet to remove the nine side-cover bolts and side cover. Keep all detents and shifter shafts in the cover. Simply lift both forks out of the case. Bag and tag shift forks for future use.

2 Remove Front Bearing Retainer

Use a 1/2-inch socket and ratchet to remove the four bolts that fasten the front bearing retainer to the case.

3 Take Off Snap Ring Spacer

Remove maindrive snap ring using snap-ring pliers and slide the spacer off the mainshaft.

4 Remove Mainshaft Bearing

Some front bearings will slide off the input shaft; others may have to be pried off. If prying is required, you can use large screwdrivers or angled pry bars as prying tools.

5 Drive Out Reverse Lock Pin

The reverse shifter shaft lock pin must be punched out from the bottom. Use a hammer and a zero size punch and carefully drive the pin out toward the top side of the case. This is a tapered pin and can ruin the case if removed in the wrong direction.

6 Pull Shifter Out of Housing

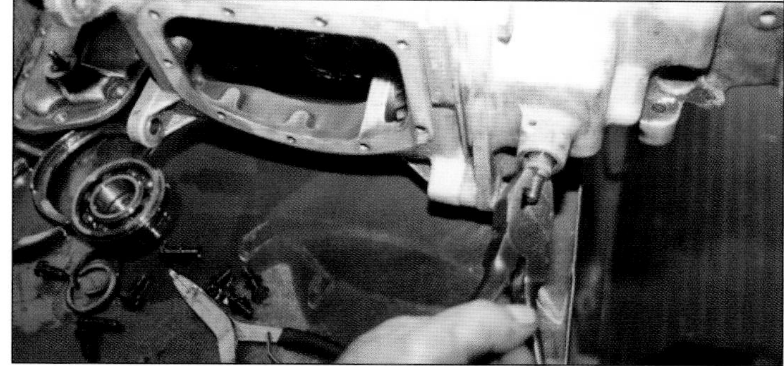

Use a pair of pliers to pull the shifter shaft out and then disengage the reverse fork from the reverse gear. Be careful not to damage the shifter shaft threads. Sometimes it is better to leave the nut on the shaft and pull on the nut.

7 Separate Tailhousing from Main Housing

Once the tailhousing bolts are removed, carefully pull the tailhousing away from the maincase. When you separate these components, the rear reverse idler gear may fall out. Some T10 transmissions have the lower two 5/8-inch bolts through the bolt into the main case. Others have them only bolt to the mid plate.

8 Pull Mainshaft Out of Housing

Pry the mid plate away from the main case and pull the mainshaft assembly out using a screwdriver or small pry bars. Some versions have a retaining bolt that has to be removed first.

Documentation Required

9 Remove 3-4 Gear Synchro Assembly

There are only two snap rings that hold the whole geartrain together. Using a snap-ring pliers, remove the 3-4 synchro snap ring first. Once the 3-4 snap ring has been removed, slide off the 3-4 synchro assembly, third gear, 2-3 thrust washer, and second gear. To make assembly easier, make sure to properly identify and store the parts.

10 Press Off 1-2 Gear Synchro and Parts

Disengage the rear snap ring using snap-ring pliers and move it out of the groove toward reverse gear. As you support the remaining parts on the 1-2 synchro, you can press the mainshaft through the 1-2 synchro, 1st gear, rear bearing, and reverse gear. Some T-10s may have a plastic speedo gear held on with a clip. This clip is simply pressed off by hand. If you have a steel speedo gear, you need to press the shaft through that gear as well.

Gear Synchros and Mainshaft Assembly

Here is a top view of how you can simply disassemble the mainshaft in two sections. You can see the order of the mainshaft gears and synchro rings.

11 Remove Rear Bearing from Assembly

Spread the snap ring open with snap-ring pliers to remove the rear bearing. Sometimes the bearing drops out; other times a hammer is required to lightly tap the bearing out. Remove input shaft and parts.

12 Remove Input Shaft

Lift out the input shaft and the forward-reverse idler gear and thrust from the main case, and pick out any loose needles and parts.

13 Punch Countershaft Out of Case

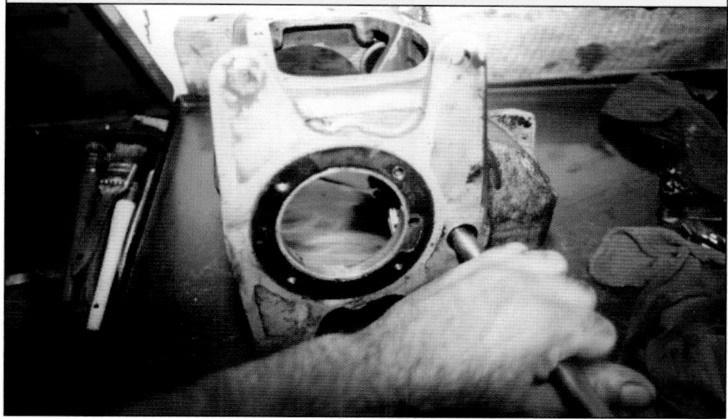

Punch the countershaft out of the case from the front toward the back. This also knocks out the woodruff key located in the rear of the case.

14 Take Out Countergear and Thrust Washers

Lift out the countergear and thrust washers from the main case. Needles in the countergear typically need to be replaced. New needles and spacers are in most rebuild kits, including a countershaft. The spacer tube is not included, so don't lose it or throw it away.

Professional Mechanic Tip PRO TIP

15 Remove Reverse Fork from Tailhousing

The reverse fork is the only part you need to remove in the tail. It just pulls off the reverse arm by hand. I leave the reverse shifter shaft in the tail. The reverse shifter shaft can be pushed toward the outside with your hands to expose the O-ring seal, so it can be changed without having to disengage the shafts' detent ball and spring.

16 Remove Shifter Shaft

The last step of the disassembly and the first step of the assembly is the side cover. Remove the shifter shafts, change the O-rings, clean the cover, and put it back together. This keeps the small detents and interlock from getting lost.

Order of Parts for the Interlock System

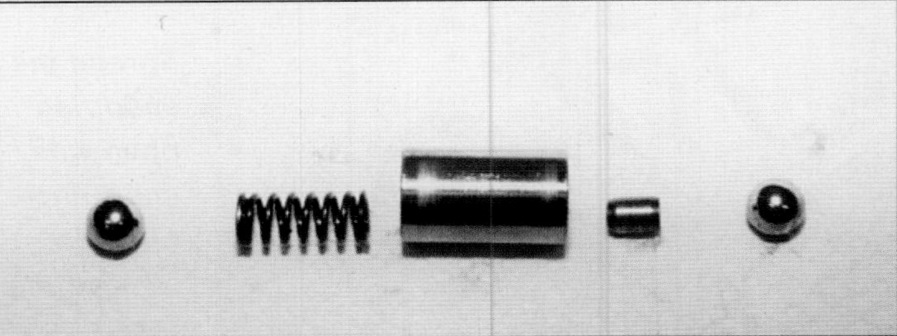

Here is how the interlock system stacks in all T10 and Super T10 4-speeds: The balls, spring, and small pin are your detents. The large tube they fit in is actually the interlock.

T10 Assembly

1 Install 1-2 Synchro Gear Assembly

Start your assembly by placing the 1-2 synchro assembly without the bronze rings on the mainshaft and the first-speed gear sleeve.

2 Slide First-Gear Parts onto Mainshaft

To assemble the transmission, you basically reverse the disassembly process. Add the new first-gear synchro ring, first gear, and rear bearing retainer with a new bearing, and then replace the snap ring. Some parts may slide back into place; others may have to be pressed on. Rebuild kits have selective fit rings, and you fit the largest ring you can in the groove. Then slide on the reverse gear and press the speedometer drive gear. That completes the back portion.

3 Install Second-Gear Parts

Professional Mechanic Tip

PRO TIP

T10s have a common second-gear jump-out problem. I replaced the second gear and also added a new 1-2 torque lock slider. To assemble, add the second gear ring, second gear, 2-3 thrust washer, third gear, third-gear synchro ring, and the 3-4 synchro assembly.

Precision Measurement

4 Install Springs in Synchro Assembly

Early T10s use a hollow stamped strut key. The tang of the spring fits inside the key. The spring on the opposite side has its tang located in the same key, but it loads in the opposite direction to give proper balance. Use this method for both synchro assemblies. Shown here is the 3-4 synchro assembly. Use a selective snap ring that gives you endplay between third and second gear between 0.010 and 0.030 inch. Try to keep toward the tighter spec.

Professional Mechanic Tip

5 Position Reverse Fork

Use assembly lube to hold the reverse idler thrust washer and reverse fork in place and shift it into the forward position, so it's easier to connect it with the reverse gear. Notice that I've lubed the reverse-shifter-shaft O-ring as well. Pull the shifter shaft outward with your hand to replace the O-ring, rather than removing it and having to deal with assembling the detent ball and spring.

6 Orient Case Face-Down for Assembly

Lay the case face-down with the countergear installed. The input shaft is in place without the front bearing, with the pilot needles loaded. In addition, the forward-reverse idler and thrust washer are in the proper position.

7 Install Mainshaft Assembly and Tailhousing

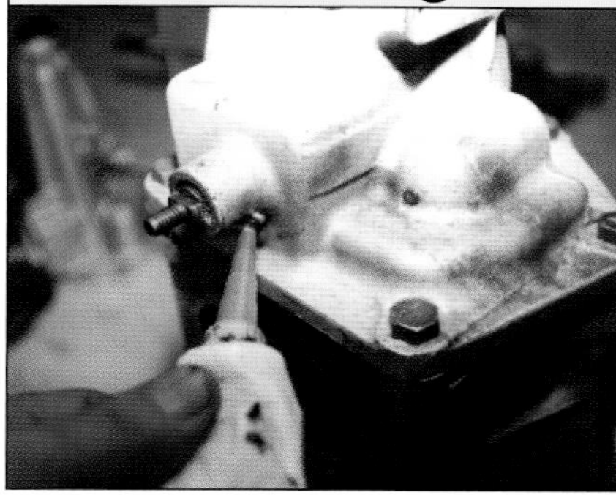

Reverse the procedure for installing the mainshaft assembly and tailhousing. The procedures are similar to the Muncie and Super T10 4-speeds. Apply assembly lube on reverse-shifter-shaft O-ring before tapping it toward reverse gear. Install tail bolts and speedo fitting, and make sure to put a drop of sealant on the reverse-shifter-shaft tapered lock pin.

8 Install New Front Bearing and Parts

Install the new front bearing by tapping it down into place with a punch. Some bearings simply drop into place. Next install the snap-ring washer, and fit the largest snap ring that you can in the snap-ring groove.

9 Bolt On Front Bearing Retainer

Install the front bearing retainer and make sure you apply sealant to the four bolts. GM T10s have no front seal, while Fords and AMCs do. So make sure to replace the seal as well. Most old seals easily pry out, an old socket can be used to press a new seal into place.

10 Install New Shift Forks

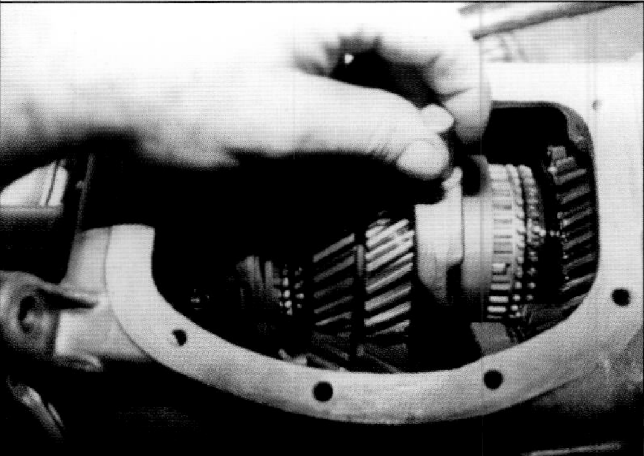

It is a good idea to replace the shift forks with new ones. New forks help ensure the transmission does not fall out of gear. The transmission is shifted into second gear before the side cover is installed. Install the remaining 3-4 shift fork and side cover, and you are done.

Rebuilding Super T10 4-Speeds

As mentioned before, the Super T10 disassembles are similar to the T10 and Muncie 4-speed. The main difference is the sequence for removing the mainshaft and gears without using special pullers. Muncie and T10 mainshafts with all the gears intact can simply be pulled out.

In contrast, the ST10 has an upper third gear that cannot clear the lower countergear, but there are two ways around this problem. The first option is to remove the front bearing, which allows you to raise the mainshaft while attached to the input shaft over the countergear and take the whole upper assembly out. This technique requires a special puller to yank the front bearing off.

The second option is easier: Remove the countershaft and allow the countergear to drop down and away from the upper mainshaft. Once the countergear is dropped, remove the mainshaft and press the input shaft out through the front bearing using the case as a support. With some ratios, you are able to remove the input shaft with the front bearing attached from the inside, allowing you to firmly press it off using a hydraulic press.

ST10 Disassembly

1 Remove Front Bearing Retainer

Take off the front bearing retainer and the side cover by removing the nine mounting bolts. Simply lift the shift forks out of the case. Before removing the tailhousing, use a hammer and punch to drive out the tapered pin from the bottom. Once removed, pull the reverse shifter shaft outward to disengage the reverse fork from the reverse gears. Unbolt and separate the tailhousing from the main case.

2 Remove Reverse Idler Shaft

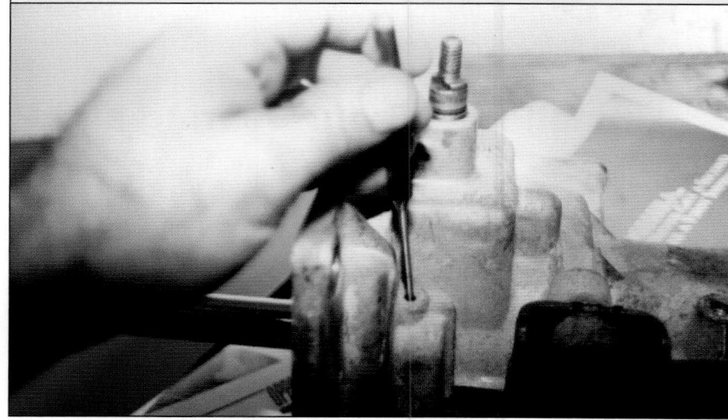

You rarely need to remove the reverse idler shaft because it seldom shows any sign of wear. If you do need to remove it, use a hammer and punch to drive the retaining pin cover and pin into the shaft.

3 Reverse Idler Shaft

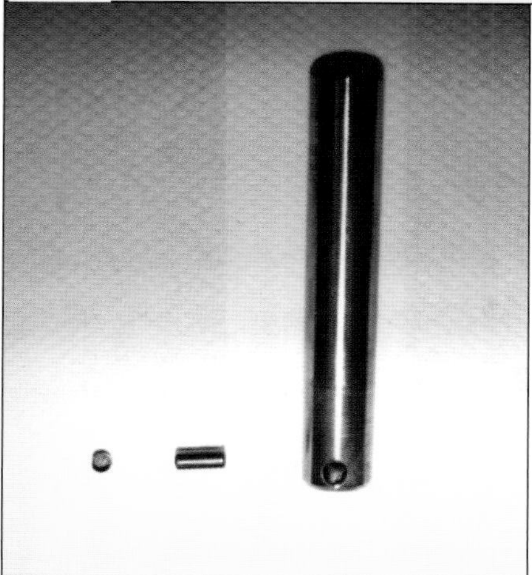

This is what the reverse idler shaft, pin, and pin cover look like when removed. To replace the shaft, simply insert the shaft back in the tail and punch the pin and pin cover in place from the outside. Apply sealant to the pin bore.

4 Remove Mainshaft Assembly

With the tail and reverse idler removed, unbolt the mid-plate retaining bolt and punch the mid plate's locating dowel into the case to remove it. Once the dowel has been removed, you can rotate the plate to expose the countershaft, so the shaft can be removed. Once the shaft has been removed, the whole geartrain has enough room to come out of the case.

5 Press Off Front Bearing

Once the input shaft has been removed, use an old wrist pin as a press arbor and press off the front bearing. Here, I'm using an old case to support the gear.

6 Replace Reverse Shifter Shaft O-Ring

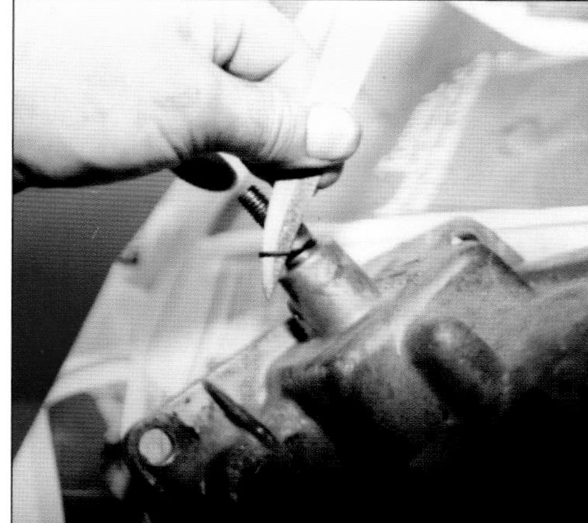

It is not necessary to remove the reverse shifter shaft to change the O–ring seal. Push it all the way out, change the O-ring, and carefully push it back in a little.

7 Remove 3-4 Synchro Snap Ring

Use a snap-ring pliers to remove the 3-4 synchro snap ring. Slide off or gently tap with a rubber mallet to remove the third gear and the 3-4 synchro assembly from the main shaft.

8 Remove Reverse Gear from Mainshaft

Remove all snap rings, speedometer drive gear, and reverse gear from the mainshaft. With the rear bearing snap ring removed, support second gear with a press clamp and press the mainshaft through second gear, the 1-2 synchro assembly, first gear, first-gear sleeve, and the rear-bearing retainer in one step.

Mainshaft Parts

The basic components of the mainshaft have been disassembled, so you can see all the major parts.

9 Remove Rear Bearing

Spread the retaining ring with snap-ring pliers and tap the rear bearing out while keeping the ring spread open.

Professional Mechanic Tip

PRO TIP

10 Press Out Countershaft

The countershaft usually fits tightly in the Super T10, and I recommend using a shop press to remove it because driving it with a hammer and drift can spread the end. The countergear is loaded like the Muncie, and it has a spacer tube, four rows of needle bearings, and six spacer rings. Load the countergear with the spacer tube, spacer ring, needle row, spacer ring, needle row, and then spacer ring. Once this has been completed, flip the gear around and add a spacer ring, needle row, spacer ring, needle row, and sixth spacer ring. The outside rings should be recessed slightly in the gear.

11 Check Countershaft for Binding

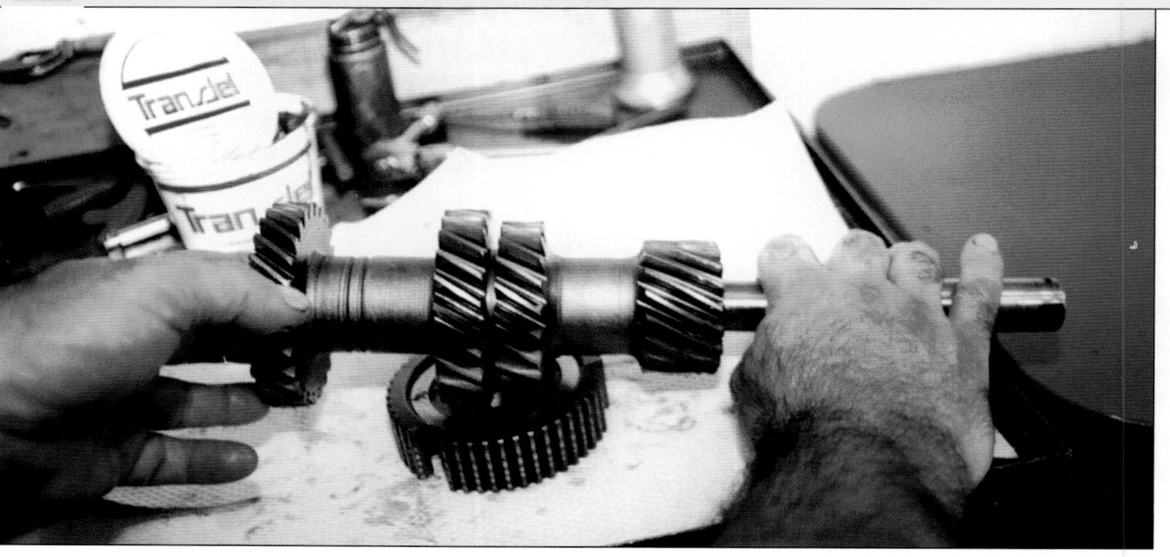

Pre-fit your countershaft in the countergear. Turn the shaft in the gear to check for rough spots because some shafts could have dings on them. Dings can be removed with a file. This procedure also aids in packing the needles.

ST10 Assembly

1 Install Countergear

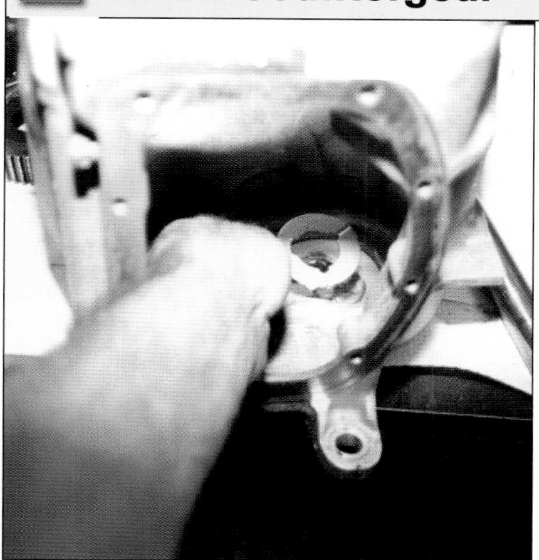

Install the forward countergear thrust washer to start the reassembly process. Use assembly lube to hold the washer in place.

2 Insert Countergear in Case

With the main case facing down, insert the countergear. I'm holding the front spacer ring with my index finger, which keeps the needles from sliding out.

3 Install Remaining Thrust Washer

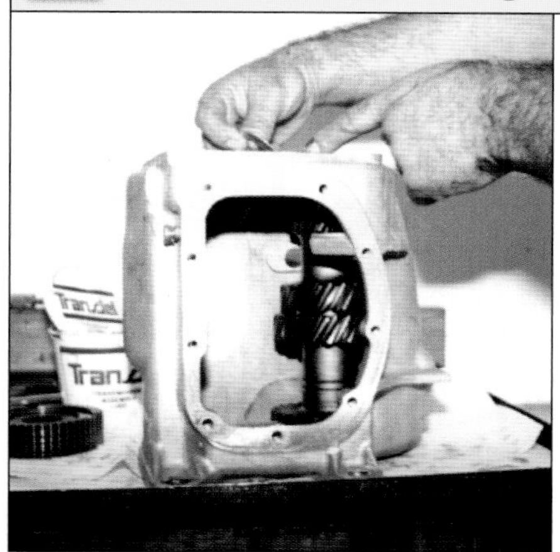

Once the countergear is in position, slide in the rear thrust washer and engage its tab in the slot in the case.

4 Position Countershaft in Case

Sink the countershaft far enough down by hand to make sure all the thrust washers line up. Press it back in place and stop about 3/8 inch before the final press and add the woodruff key. Then sink it home.

5 Load Needles into Input Shaft

The input shaft needles look like this when loaded in place.

6 Insert Input Shaft into Case

Drop the input shaft in place without the front bearing. The whole front case subassembly is facing down, and an old front case supports it. Add the forward reverse idler and its thrust washer and the fourth-gear synchro ring.

7 Slide Second Gear and 1-2 Assembly onto Mainshaft

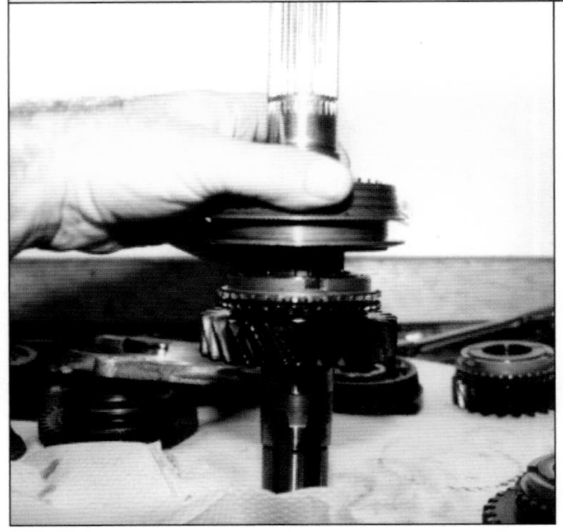

Slide second gear and the 1-2 assembly onto the mainshaft to start assembly. Notice the direction of the slider. The hub's protruding edge is facing second gear.

8 Press First Gear onto Mainshaft

Flip the assembly around and press on the first-gear bushing. Some will slide on, but most require a mild press.

9 Install First Gear onto Mainshaft

Flip the shaft around and slide the first-gear synchro ring, first gear, and first-gear thrust washer.

10 Install Rear Bearing and Retainer

Drop into place or lightly tap down the rear-bearing retainer with a new rear bearing. Tap it down with a hammer and punch until it feels snug. When down all the way the snap-ring groove will be exposed.

Precision Measurement

11 Install Rear Bearing Snap Ring

Make sure the rear-bearing's 0.062-inch-thick snap-ring washer is installed first, and then fit in the thickest selective snap ring in your rebuild kit. The thickest ring will remove all endplay.

12 Install Reverse Gear

Install the reverse sliding gear, forward speedo gear snap ring, speedo drive gear, and rear speedo gear snap ring. These two snap rings are usually 0.087-inch thick.

13 Install Third Gear

Install third gear, third-gear synchro ring, 3-4 synchro assembly, and its snap ring. Usually this ring is 0.087- to 0.091-inch thick. Always use a 0.087-inch one here. The last part is the needle-bearing thrust spacer. Hold this in place with grease. Notice the direction of the slider and hub.

14 Main Case Rear Gasket

Assemble the ST10 with the main case on top of an old main case. Apply a small bead of sealant to hold the gasket in place and form a perfect seal.

15 Preposition the 3-4 Slider

Before installing the mainshaft assembly, pull the 3-4 slider forward on the shaft. This allows the mainshaft to clear the countergear when installed in the case. Be careful not to let the strut keys fly out.

Important!

16 Install Mainshaft Assembly

This picture shows why the 3-4 hub is pulled forward to clear the countergear. I've reinstalled the dowel in the mid plate and will carefully mate the mainshaft to the input shaft. Make sure you line the fourth-gear synchro ring key slots with the strut keys before dropping the whole assembly in place.

Torque Fasteners

17 Install Retaining Bolt

Once the mid plate is sitting flush, tighten the retaining bolt to 30 ft-lbs.

18 Install Rear Reverse Idler Gear

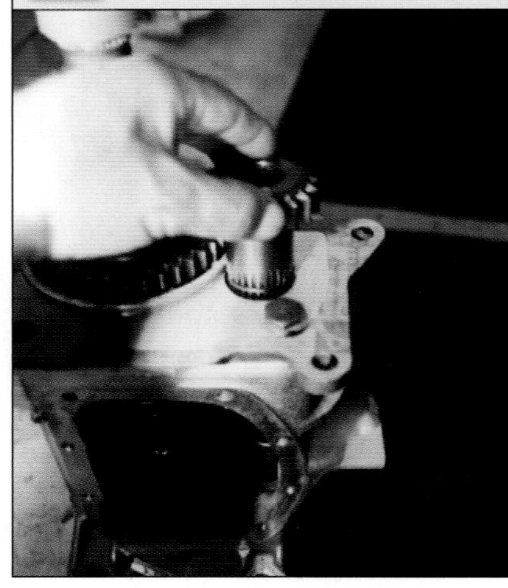

You really have to use a combination of RTV sealant and gaskets on this transmission because the two lower bolts never enter the main case. This area can warp because the main case does not support it.

19 Insert Reverse Fork

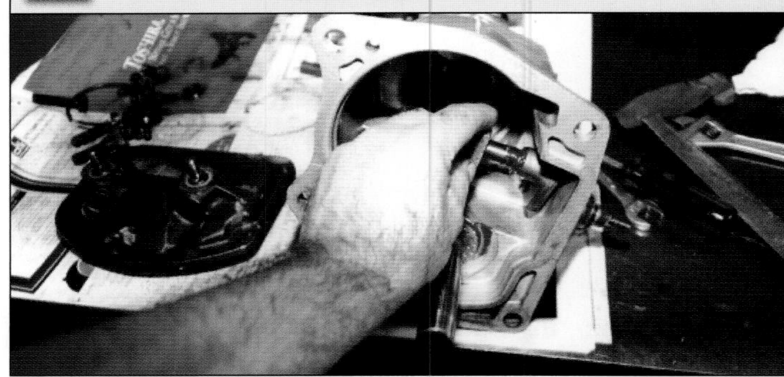

Install the reverse idler shaft and thrust washer. Insert the reverse fork. Everything is held in place with assembly lube. Note that the reverse shifter shaft is moved forward in the reverse position.

Professional Mechanic Tip

20 Lower Tailhousing onto Main Case

By applying pressure with my palm, I'm holding up the reverse gear with my fingers and holding the reverse fork against the reverse gear. You catch the fork onto the reverse gear and gently lower the tailhousing in place, then push the reverse shifter shaft back in place.

Torque Fasteners

21 Fasten Tailhousing to Mid Plate

Once the tailhousing is flush with the mid plate, torque it down to 30 ft-lbs. Clean off excess sealant to give the build a "professional" appearance. Remember to install a new tapered pin, which should come in your rebuild kit.

22 Install Front Bearing

Install the front bearing the same way as the mid plate. Use a punch and work the bearing down while holding the input.

23 Install Outer-Case Parts

Once the bearing is in place, pull it out and install its outer-case retaining ring. Install the 0.062-inch bearing snap-ring spacer and then fit the thickest snap ring in front of it.

Torque Fasteners

24 Install Front Retainer Gasket(s)

Some bearing retainers require thicker gaskets. Our gasket sets include two front retainer gaskets. Place the bearing retainer on the transmission and use one gasket as a "feeler gauge." If you can pull the gasket out while holding the retainer against the bearing, the retainer won't seal and another gasket is required. Obviously, replace the front seal, use sealant on the four retainer bolts, bolt it up, and torque to 18 ft-lbs.

Professional Mechanic Tip

25 Install Parts in Shift Cover

More than likely the side cover will come apart when removing it. Install the shifter shaft seals first, and then install the shifter shafts with care to avoid pinching or rolling over the seals. Notice the sequence of the components. The outer sleeve is actually the interlock mechanism. The spring, balls, and pin are the detent mechanism.

26 Check Operation of Shift Cover

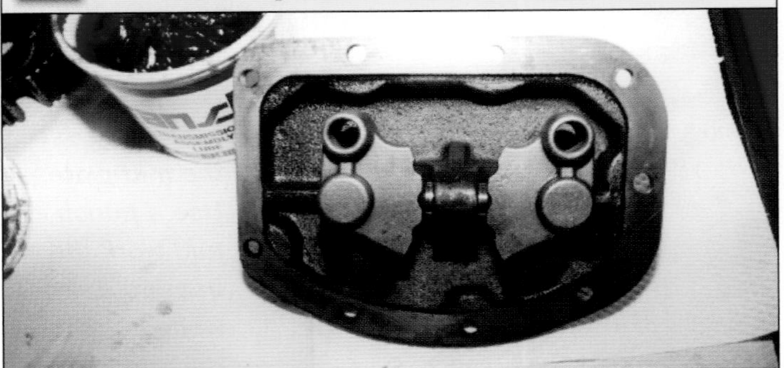

After the detents and interlock are installed, check for smooth motion. You should bolt on the linkage arms so that the mechanism can't fly apart. This is what it looks like in neutral, from the inside.

Torque Fasteners

27 Install Shift Cover

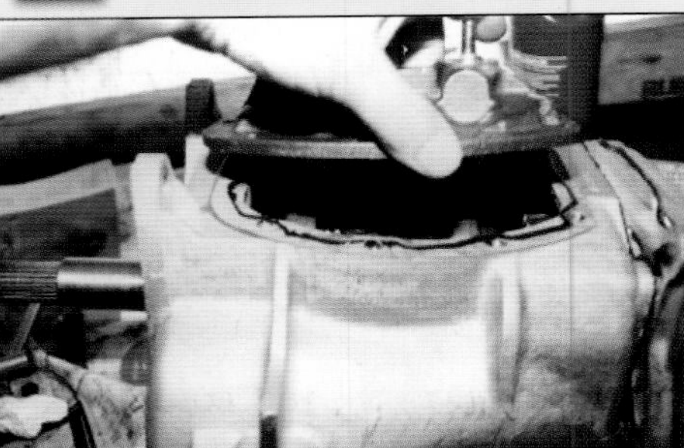

Install a bead of sealant on both sides of this side-cover gasket. The shift forks are lying on the sliders. You will have to put the transmission into second gear to get the 1-2 shift fork in place. You can leave it in second gear, but you must remember to shift the side cover into second as well. Once in place, install the nine side-cover bolts, and torque to 18 ft-lbs.

T5 5-Speed History

In 1985, I was doing a great deal of rebuilding for several new car dealers. A T5 transmission had come in with a broken third-gear section from a local Ford dealer. It was different from the normal T5s I had worked on. The first thing I noticed is that it no longer had bronze synchro rings but ones made of a fiber material similar to a clutch lining in an automatic. After doing some research and making a few calls, I found out that the T5 was upgraded to "world-class" standards.

There is a reason I placed this little bit of information first. It is important to understand that BorgWarner, the manufacturer of the T5, was notorious for making unannounced and undocumented changes to production transmissions. T10 4-speeds, SR4 4-speeds, T50 5-speeds, and T4 and T5 transmissions all had a variety of design changes during a production run. Undocumented changes can cause service nightmares and the generation of misinformation. These changes are usually for the better. As certain designs fail when put into a production environment, new improvements are created to remedy warranty issues.

The T5 evolved from the T4, which evolved from the SR4 4-speed. The SR4/T5 concept was a departure from conventional T50 5-speed design. The SR4 stood for "Single Rail 4-speed." The T50 5-speed used three rails. In fact, BorgWarner seemed to be the only company continuing to design single-rail shifting transmissions. Tremec did make the SROD (Single Rail Over Drive), but this design had many flaws, and new units went back to the three-rail system. When I researched the patents on the T5, it was interesting to find out that patents were approved for the fiber-lined synchro rings and single-rail shifting mechanisms in 1981.

In a three-rail system, the shifter is connected to a shift rail, which selects three other rails, such as the 1-2, 3-4, and 5-reverse rails. In a single-rail system, one rail rotates and, by use of shift lugs, shifts individual 1-2, 3-4, 5-reverse synchros. The single-rail design, if implemented correctly, produces a lighter shifting mechanism as well as a very positive shift movement and feel. By using lightweight components, such as powdered metal interlocks and aluminum shift forks, shifting is much quicker.

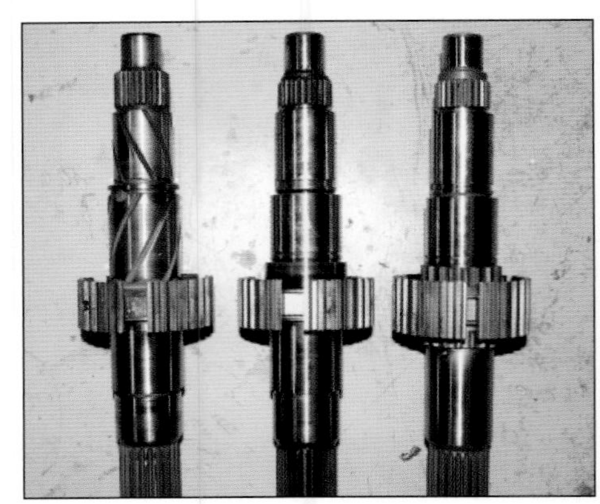

From the left are: T5 NWC mainshaft, hybrid NWC mainshaft with roller bearing surface, and WC mainshaft.

Both the NWC bronze ring (left) and the lined WC ring (right) shown here are 3-4 rings.

The early non-world-class (NWC) T5s used a combination of flat roller bearings and thrust washers on the countergear. The input and output shafts used tapered cup-and-cone bearings. This design seemed to be influenced by the SR4 and T50, which both used a combination of flat roller bearings and thrust washers. By the nature of their design, flat roller/thrust washer systems cannot allow for preload. This allows gears to move around and get out of mesh.

The T5 transmission has many variations and is exported to China, Korea, and Europe for use in foreign vehicles.

While many people assume the T5 only came in Ford and GM variations, it was actually offered in many different spline configurations. Here is a large selection of T5 input shafts.

Non-world-class boxes used all-bronze synchro rings. The world-class version allows for preload because it uses tapered bearings on the countergear as well. The drawback is that you have to use shims to set endplay or preload, and that requires more time. The world-class T5 uses fiber composite synchro rings on all gears except fifth. This is similar to material used in automatic transmission friction plates. All speed gears in world-class boxes ride on needle bearings except for fifth gear. This concept produces less parasitic drag and improves shift response. The use of fiber synchro rings and tighter tolerances requires lighter weight oils, such as Dextron III. Use of conventional gear lubes will ruin these transmissions.

The world-class spec did not replace the non-world-class design. In fact, both designs were produced at the same time. It boils down to how much money manufacturers wanted to spend. T5s were used in General Motors, Ford, AMC, TVR, Cosworth, Izuzu, Australian Holdens, Korean SSANGS, Nissan, Nisson, and Panther cars as well as Jacobson tractors and several utility vehicles. Beijing Warner in China also manufactured the transmission for Beijing Jeep. As of this writing, there are more than 260 T5 assembly part numbers.

T5 identification questions are common. It ranks number one in my popularity poll. So far, the basic T5 has been produced for 26 years, from 1982 to present. With so many variations available, it has become very popular for a multitude of projects and conversions.

Rebuilding the T5

There are several variations of the T5. Besides having the world-class and non-world-class specs, there are subtle changes in the world-class spec itself. The buildups cover world-class transmissions because of their current popularity. You may have heard of "Cobra"-style T5s, which have a tapered bearing in the input shaft as opposed to flat rollers. Some also have a reverse brake, which acts as synchro for reverse gear. T5s do not use any gaskets. The factory used black RTV, but I recommend Permatex 51813. A rebuild kit is a must for a T5 because individual components tend to cost as much as a whole kit. Variations are covered in the build up.

Too much sealant can get lodged in the housing bolt bores. When you screw in the bolts, hydraulic action may blow the case apart, especially if you use air tools.

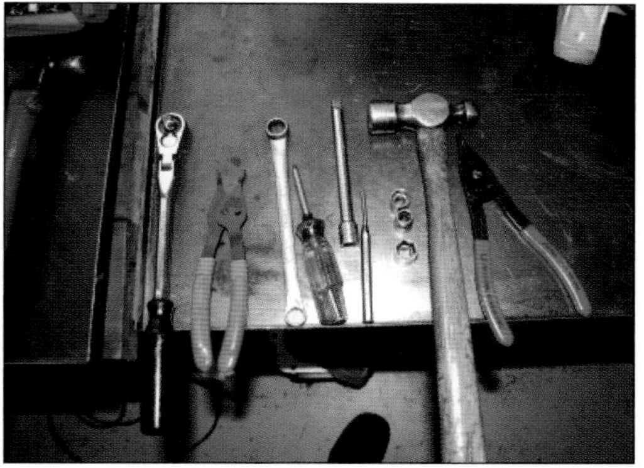

These are the very basic tools needed for a T5 build up. Access to a hydraulic press and a bearing clamp are necessary.

T5 Disassembly

1 Remove Shifter-Cover Bolts

Remove the four shifter-cover bolts and pry off the shifter. Jeep units have five bolts.

2 Remove Dowel Pin for Lever

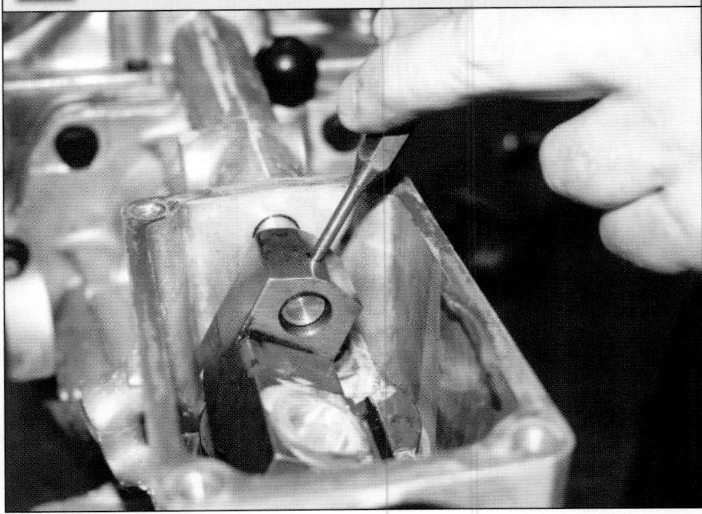

Punching down the offset lever dowel pin disengages the lever from the rail.

3 Properly Store Shifter Parts

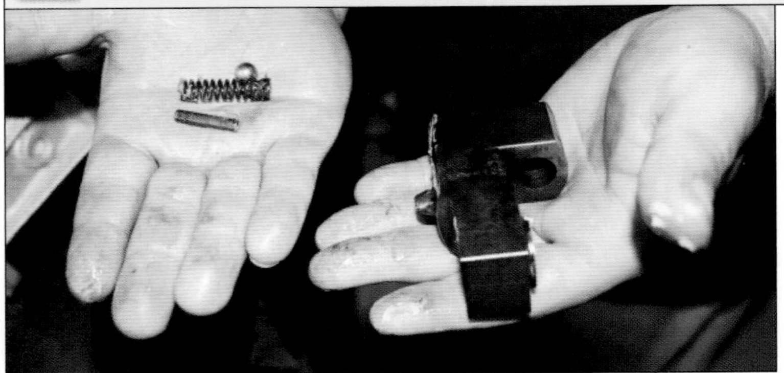

Make sure the pin is completely removed from the lever, and all components are stored in the parts tray.

4 Separate Tailhousing from Main Case

Remove the tailhousing's bolts, pry the tail off, and remove the tail and offset lever in one step. Bolts have a 15-mm head. Be careful not to lose the detent ball and spring.

5 Remove Top-Cover Bolts and Cover

Remove all the 10-mm cover bolts. Using a screwdriver to pry on the top cover to break the sealant bond. Some covers have pry tabs cast in; for others you have to pry carefully between the case and the cover.

6 Remove Front Bearing Retainer

Remove the four 13-mm front retainer bolts and pry the retainer off. There are special recessed pry areas below the bearing retainer on the case so you don't damage sealing surfaces.

Precision Measurement

7 Measure Front Bearing Race and Shims

The front bearing race and shims are inside the retainer. Make sure you take a thickness measurement. If the shims have not been damaged, the same shim can be reused. Also, the original shim size makes a good starting point when beginning fresh with new gears.

8 Remove Input Shaft and Parts

Remove the input by pulling it out of the front of the case. Rotate and pull at the same time to clear the lower countergear. Also extract the fourth-gear synchro ring and any flat thrust washers.

9 Remove Needles and Flat Roller Plate

Remove all loose needles and the flat roller and store them safely. Some needles may fall out into the case.

Main Needles for T5

The three types of main drive needles in T5 transmissions are: (from the left) 15 needles and a spacer, a caged roller found in most European T5s, a tapered cup, and a cone bearing in later-Cobra-style Ford T5s.

10 Drive Out Fifth-Gear Fork Pin

Support the fifth-gear fork with a socket, and drive out the fork's roll pin with a hammer.

11 Remove Fifth-Gear Assembly

Flip the transmission on its face. This makes it easy to remove the fifth-speed assembly snap ring and pry off the assembly and fork. Pry between the fifth gear and the case.

Fifth-Gear Synchro Retainers

The left fifth-speed synchro retainer is a standard T5 type. The one on the right is the reverse brake style.

12 Remove Fifth-Gear and Reverse Rail

With the fifth-gear fork and synchro assembly out (1), you can remove the lower fifth gear (2) and rear mainshaft bearing race (3).

Professional Mechanic Tip

13 Prep for Mainshaft Removal

The 0.80-inch OD sets and aftermarket fifth gears are larger than the rear bearing race. You can't remove the rear race and mainshaft. It is next to impossible to remove upper fifth gears with a puller, so I drop the countergear, push the upper gear train in the case, and cut the bearing race in to spots 180 degrees apart. This allows me to gain the clearance needed to remove and lift the mainshaft out of the case once the rear race is gone.

14 Lift Mainshaft from Case

Once the mainshaft bearing race has been removed, you can lift the geartrain out of the top. Notice that you don't need to mess with the fifth-reverse lever.

15 Remove Speedometer Drive

Press on the clip to release the speedometer drive gear. Here, the inset shows later-model speedometer reluctors, which also act as a secondary retainer for fifth gear. You must remove the reluctor first, before removing the fifth-speed snap ring.

Important!

16 Press Gears Off

Never try pulling fifth gear off or using press clamps against it. Use press plates to support under first gear (where you can get optimum support), and press first through the upper fifth off.

All these parts will come off in one action by using a press.

17 Remove Gears and Bearings

Flip the geartrain around, support with press clamps under third gear, and press the mainshaft through the 3-4 synchro and third gear. Units with the Cobra pocket bearing require you to press under the bearing first, remove the bearing, then remove the 3-4 synchro snap ring before doing this step.

Here are all the parts that come off the mainshaft when this step has been performed.

18 Remove Second Gear and Parts

Remove the second-gear retaining ring, thrust washer, second gear, bearing, and bearing spacer.

Laying the parts out on a bench in the order in which they were removed helps you to reassemble it more easily.

19 Remove Second Gear Thrust Washer and Synchro Ring

Use a small screwdriver to start unwrapping the spiral lock retaining ring that holds the second-gear thrust washer and synchro ring in place.

20 Take Off 1-2 Slider

Sometimes the 1-2 slider falls off from the first gear side. It is the final part to slide off; don't lose the keys and springs. My finger is holding a small pin, which keeps the first-gear sleeve from spinning. Don't lose that either. Later units use a tiny ball bearing. So be careful.

Professional Mechanic Tip

21 Remove Countergear Parts and Press Off Rear Bearings

Remove the four countergear retaining-plate bolts, the plate, and shim. Use your press clamps to clamp under the rear bearing. This elevates the countergear just enough to press it through the rear bearing. Use an aluminum drift on the back side of the counter to press it off.

22 Remove Countergear from Main Case

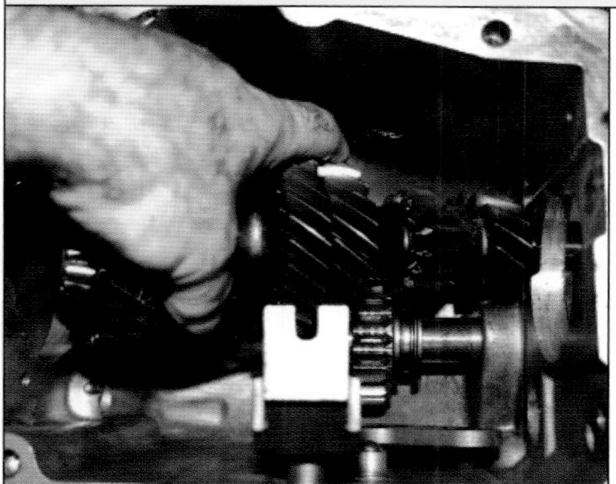

Once the rear bearing is removed, the countergear comes out of the main case. Again, notice that the fifth-reverse lever was never removed.

23 Break Off Counterbearing

There is no way to remove the front countergear bearing without destroying it. So I break off the cage of the bearing with a screwdriver, which gives me a solid lip for fastening my press clamps.

Professional Mechanic Tip

24 Press Off Gear

Support the gear on an old transmission case and press it through the front bearing race with an old idler shaft. Now both bearings are removed from the countergear. Your T5 is now completely apart.

Now that the T5 is more than 20 years old, some units may have already been rebuilt or assembled with a variety of parts. With more than 265 T5 models, you can mix-and-match cases and gearsets to a point. If colored sealants (red, blue, or clear) have been used, it's tell-tale sign that the T5 has been taken apart.

It is not necessary to completely disassemble a T5. The top cover need not be disassembled and lower countergear need not be removed unless these components in the cover, the countergear, or its bearings need replacement.

There are several procedures that you may or may not have to do. The first optional procedure is to remove the reverse idler gear and shaft, which are simply held in with a roll pin. The other is removing the front countergear bearing or front input shaft bearing since these bearings actually never fail. If the countergear isn't broken, you may want to leave the whole gear still in the case and avoid that step altogether, if for example, you are just changing synchro rings.

T5 Assembly From the Ground Up

In my shop, we deburr all the gears in the T5s we build. If they are used for heavy-duty street/strip use, we add one of our countergear stabilizer plates. We designed the plate to keep preloads constant as well as add steel support for the rear-countergear bearing race. Aluminum copies really don't accomplish anything and are a waste of money. The T5 requires only two measurements for assembly. I've found that if you preload the countergear with 4 to 6 inch-pounds of drag, and you keep the upper geartrain to more than 0.003-inch to zero endplay, you will extend the life of your T5 compared to factory specs, which call for endplay.

T5 Assembly

1 Apply Sealant to Front Countergear Bore

Starting with the bare case, use Permatex 51813 sealant to coat the front countergear bearing bore. The fifth-reverse shift rail Welch plug does not need to be removed. However, if it was removed, now is a good time to reinstall it.

Important!

2 Install Front Countergear Bearing Cup

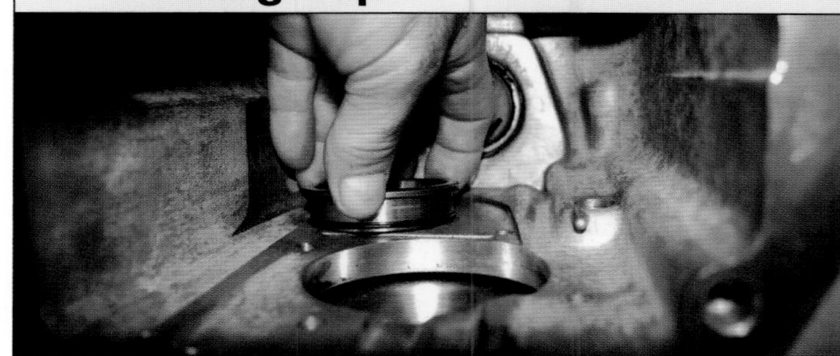

Install the front bearing cup carefully. Seat it by hand first then tap it in gently to avoid ripping the O-ring.

3 Install Fifth-Reverse Shift Arm and Clip

Install the fifth-reverse shift arm and clip. The pin that it rides on doesn't have to be removed, but if you do remove it, reinstall it with red liquid thread locker.

4 Install Reverse Idler Gear and Parts

For clarity I removed the fifth-reverse arm. Install the reverse idler, O-ring, and idler shaft, and pin it back in place. Install the roll pin so it is centered in the shaft.

5 Install Countergear

Press on the front countergear bearing using a simple socket and hammer. Remember to place the rear bearing on the countergear after it is installed in the main case.

Simply tap the bearing on with a small punch slowly, and work evenly from side to side. Yes, a long pipe would work as well, but for the one-time rebuild, this works fine.

Retainer Plates

Here are a standard retainer plate (left) and our beefed-up stabilizer (right). I have found that under heavy load, the factory plate stretches and that allows for the countergear to move around too much. It is not needed for a standard rebuild. I designed this plate to be made of steel; cheap copies made of aluminum will not work.

6 Install Countergear Shim

I'm using a 0.132-inch-thick shim here. Lately I seem to average 0.125 to 0.135 inch. Our new Peel-'n-Place shims use a solid 0.090-inch shim and a peelable 0.080-inch shim in 0.005-inch increments.

7 Install Retaining Plate

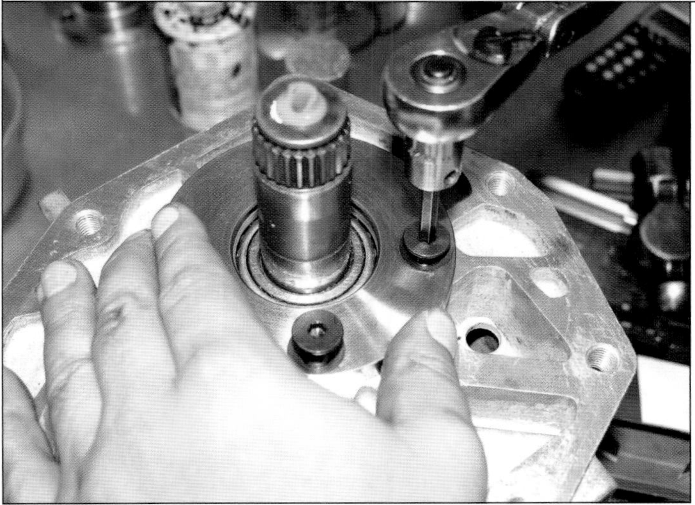

Whatever plate you decide to use, shim it to yield 4 to 6 inch-pounds of drag. Use an inch-pounds torque wrench to measure this. If you're doing it by "feel," the counter-gear should have no endplay and some smooth drag to it.

8 Clean Up Shift Rails

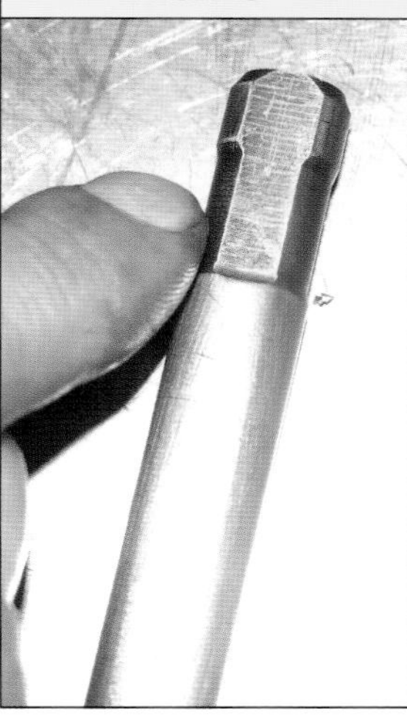

Deburr and polish all shift rails. These rails have a tendency to get chewed up from dirt in the case bores.

9 Reverse Fork Installation

Variation A: *Insert reverse idler fork, return spring, and insert rail. Once in place, turn the rail so the roller engages the fork.* Variation B: *This should be done before any gears are in case. Insert wrap spring on fork. Slip the spring through reverse arm and fasten to case post. Once in place, insert fifth-reverse arm Torx bit shaft. Then insert reverse idler gear assembly and, finally, fifth-reverse shift rail.*

Important!

10 Locate Slider Strut Slots

Later units have specific locations for strut keys. Make sure the center key slot lines up with the key slot in the synchro hub. This applies to the 1-2 as well as the 3-4 synchro assemblies. Install the 1-2 slider with the fork groove facing toward the front and install the three strut keys and two springs.

11 Pre-lube Synchro Rings

Pre-lube the synchro rings in Dextron III fluid prior to installation. Install the second-gear ring set first.

12 Install Second Gear Thrust Washer and Retaining Ring

After installing the second-gear synchro ring, install the second-gear thrust washer and spiral lock retaining ring. A small screwdriver can do this quite well.

13 Install Second Gear and Parts

Install the second gear first, then the bearing spacer, and the needle bearing. This method prevents the tiny spacer from getting caught under the gear and bent.

14 Install 2-3 Thrust Washer and Snap Ring

Install the 2-3 thrust washer and its snap ring.

15 Install Third Gear and Parts

Install third gear and its synchro ring first, then the third-gear needle spacer, and the needle bearing.

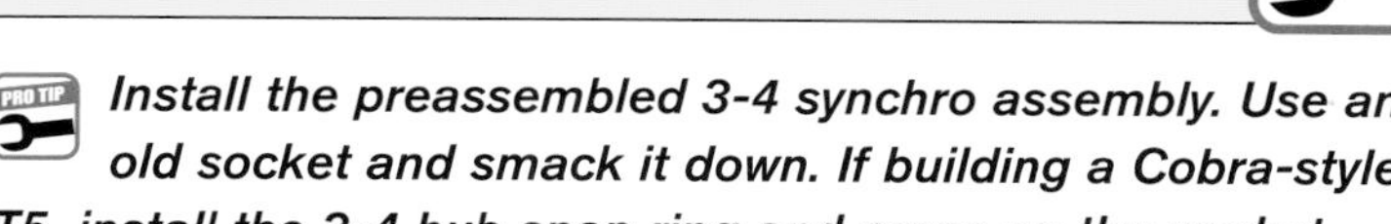

16 Install 3-4 Synchro Assembly

Install the preassembled 3-4 synchro assembly. Use an old socket and smack it down. If building a Cobra-style T5, install the 3-4 hub snap ring and press on the pocket bearing. Use a 1/2-inch socket to either press the bearing on or tap it down with a hammer. For complete synchro ring assembly instructions, refer to page 26.

17 Install First Gear Sleeve and Pin

Flip the mainshaft over and insert the first-gear sleeve anti-rotation pin by sliding it over the shaft. Right: Later units use a ball.

18 Install First Gear and Sleeve Assembly

Install the first-gear roller bearing and sleeve assembly and make sure you catch the rotation pin/ball in its slot.

19 Install First Gear and Rear Bearing

Install first gear and the rear bearing. Press on the upper fifth gear as well. If you have a 0.80-inch OD fifth gear that doesn't fit through the rear bearing race, install the mainshaft assembly in the case without the fifth gear on the shaft.

20 Install Fifth Gear

Important!

Here is the common approach to installing fifth gear. Inset: This is how you press on a fifth-speed gear when the gear does not fit through the rear bearing race. The rear bearing race is held in place with a home-made retainer. The whole transmission is fitted into the press. I'm pressing against the tip of the mainshaft.

Always install a new fifth-gear snap ring with the correct pliers. For some reason, people often leave this step out.

21 Assembled Geartrain

The completed T5 geartrain looks like this. Notice the direction the synchro sliders are facing and how the 3-4 slider's tapered edge is facing toward the front.

Fifth Gear Synchros

The fifth gear on the left shows the later-designed and stronger synchro-engagement tooth design than the gear on the right.

22 Replace Pads on All Shift Forks

These inexpensive plastic pads on the shift forks simply snap on and off and should be replaced. This stage is a good time to replace all pads on all forks.

23 Install Lower Fifth Gear and Synchro Ring

Drop the lower fifth gear and its new synchro ring in place. Install the fifth-speed fork in the fifth-gear synchro assembly, and slide the whole assembly into place. Notice the orientation of the slider, hub, and fork.

24 Install Fifth-Gear Spacer and Retaining Ring

Install the fifth-gear spacer and retaining ring. With the reverse brake variation, install the reverse synchro ring, brake cone, washer, and retaining ring. This is also a good time to install a new oil funnel.

25 Install Reverse Fork Retaining Pin

With a punch and a hammer, drive in the reverse fork retaining roll pin until it is flush with the top of the fork. Inset: The left fork is the newer style, which adds more support to the early fork on the right. New forks sell for under $20, so they are a worthy upgrade.

26 Install Speedometer Gear

There are many T5 speedometer drive-gear variations. The more common ones simply fasten with a spring clip. Others use a ball and snap ring.

27 Prepare Input Shaft for Installation

Press on the input front tapered bearing. Load the inside needles and flat roller bearing. Use assembly lube to hold them in place. Pocket bearing units simply must have a race pressed in.

28 Install Bearing on Input Shaft

If you don't have a press, gradually walk the bearing down with a punch and a hammer, tapping on the punch from side to side.

29 Insert Main Drive-Thrust Washer and Parts

Install the main drive-thrust washer and needle spacer. Some older units didn't have a spacer. It keeps the needles from skewing, so it is a good idea to install it on every unit. Pocket bearing units don't require this step or parts.

30 Slide On Fourth-Gear Synchro Ring

Install the new fourth-gear synchro ring. Hold it in place by putting assembly grease in its key slots and press it into the synchro assembly.

31 Align and Install Input Shaft

The input shaft has a clearance slot on its engagement teeth, which clears the countergear. Align the clearance space with the countergear and insert the input shaft into the main case.

Critical Inspection

32 Inspect Shift Lugs

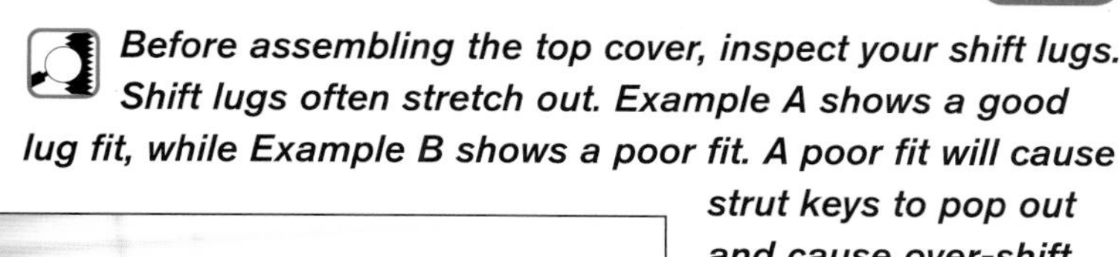

Before assembling the top cover, inspect your shift lugs. Shift lugs often stretch out. Example A shows a good lug fit, while Example B shows a poor fit. A poor fit will cause strut keys to pop out and cause over-shift issues.

Important!

33 Punch Out Shift Finger Rail Pan

Since all that is required to disassemble the top cover is to punch out the shift finger roll pin and pull it all apart, many forget how it goes back together. Notice that the 3-4 fork lug sits lower than the 1-2 fork lug. Also notice the position of the shift finger's roll pin. The front of the cover is to the left.

Important!

34 Orient Interlock Plate

Also, the location of the interlock plate is an important detail because it is very easy to install it upside down. The correct way is shown here.

35 Apply Sealant to Main Case

Apply sealant on the top of the main case, on the tailhousing for the tail section, and on the front retainer. This step ensures that sealant is not displaced during assembly, which could cause a potential leak.

36 Install Top Cover

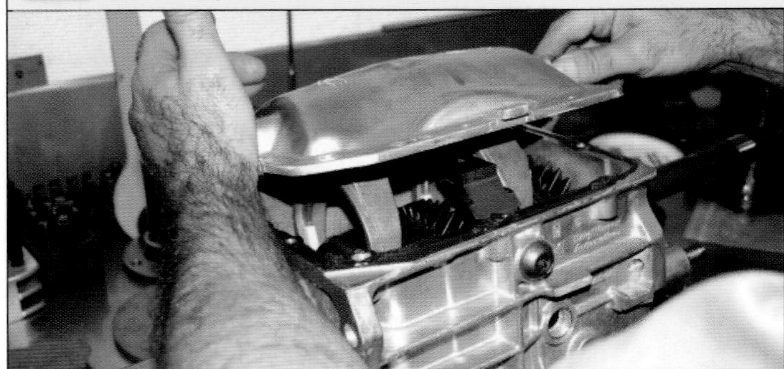

The fifth-gear-reverse arm rests on top of the other lugs. Install the top cover by moving it away from yourself to clear the fifth-reverse arm, and then toward yourself and down.

Torque Fasteners

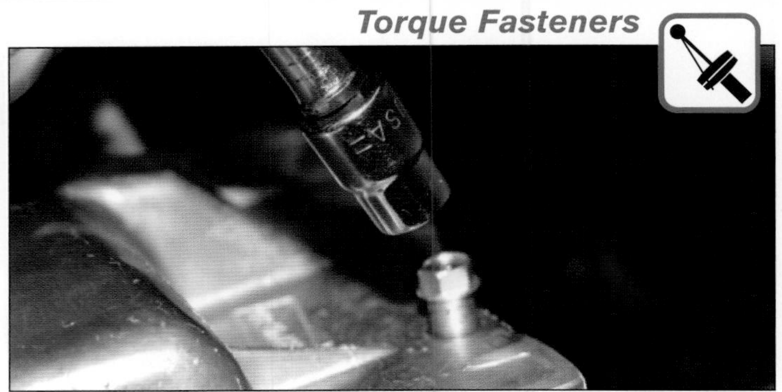

First install both dowel bolts, and then the remaining eight bolts, to fasten the cover. Torque the bolts to 12 ft-lbs.

37 Insert Detent Ball in Tailhousing Track Plate

Use assembly grease to hold the detent ball in the tailhousing's track plate.

Torque Fasteners

38 Slide Tail Assembly onto Main Case

Apply sealant to the tail, loaded the detent spring in the offset lever, and install a new shifter bushing. Both are held in place with grease. Position the offset lever's spring on the detent ball in the tail in the neutral position. Slide the tail on while applying a firm downward pressure on the offset lever. Torque the tail's eight bolts to 25 ft-lbs.

Precision Measurement

39 Shim Input Shaft

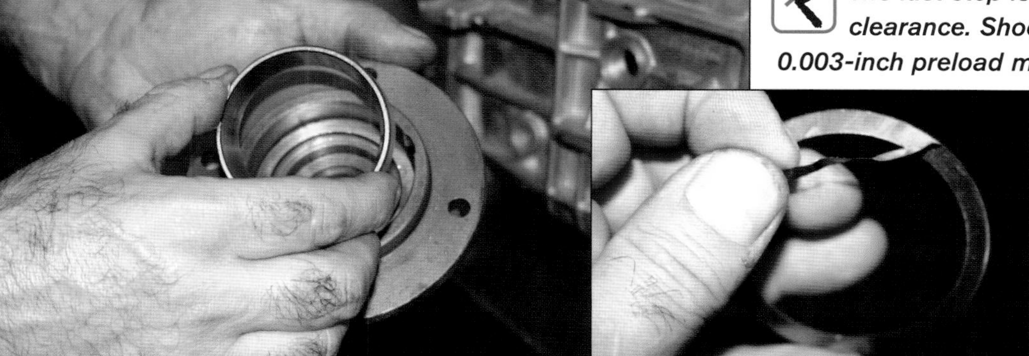

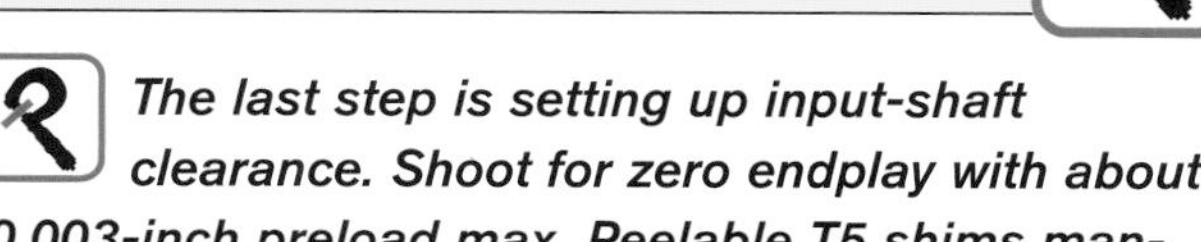

The last step is setting up input-shaft clearance. Shoot for zero endplay with about 0.003-inch preload max. Peelable T5 shims manufactured by 5speeds.com make the job a snap. Do not install the seals. Once the endplay is set, seat both input and output shafts with a rap of a rubber mallet, then recheck for endplay.

Torque Fasteners

40 Install Seals and Retainer

Once you're happy with the endplay, install the front seal, front retainer, and rear seal. Older transmissions have aluminum retainers that gall and wear fast. Upgrade to a newer cast-iron retainer. Torque the four bolts to 20 ft-lbs.

Critical Inspection

41 Check Parts and Fasteners

Final check: Tailhousing bolts are torqued and residual sealant wiped clean (1). Offset level has roll pin and shifter bushing installed (2). Front retainer bolts are installed and residual sealant is cleaned (3). Reverse light switch is installed (4).

High-Performance T5

In 1995 I thought the T5 would make a great road-racing transmission for cars up to 400 hp. To me there were plenty of transmissions rated for more than 500 hp, and I felt the use of these big transmissions in 200-hp applications would simply rob too much power. The JT5 was created for a Jaguar race team in late 1995. Jaguars required a very short transmission, so basically I shortened the T5 from 24 to 15 inches using a custom-designed mainshaft and tailhousing. It would only see 400 hp. In 10 years, who knew that because of the JT5 size, they would be installed in everything from Ferraris, Aston Martins, Volvos, Morgans, MGBs, and many other makes. The JT5 has been installed in more than 800 street Jaguars and has sparked interest in overseas companies to now make similar products based on the T5 platform.

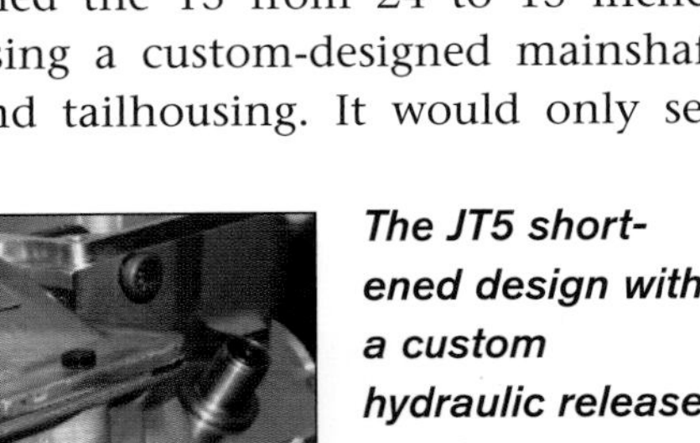

The JT5 shortened design with a custom hydraulic release bearing.

The need for better gear ratios and stronger gears led to a complete redesign, featuring dog-ring-style gears, modular countergears, and beefed-up mainshafts. All contained better grade alloys with all gears riding on needle bearings.

By 2001, G-Force Transmissions came on the scene, concentrating on the street/strip market. Its T5 is a great-shifting transmission. G-Force has made heavy-duty 9310 helical replacement gears, helical dog-ring gears, and straight-cut gears as well.

They claim that these gearsets, if set up correctly, can handle more than 500 hp.

By late 2005, Liberty's High Performance Products took over our Enduro design and made a gearset suited for drag racing. Unlike other aftermarket T5 gearsets, the Enduro mainshaft is much larger in diameter and eliminates the common areas of flex and stress. It is the only gearset that doesn't duplicate the poor factory mainshaft design.

BONUS CONTENT:
Scan to learn how to rebuild a T5 Non World Class 5-speed transmission.

The stock T5 countergear (left) and the Enduro countergear (right).

The 9310 Nickel G-Force counter-gears are machined from billet bar stock.

This is a modular helical G-Force countergear for a T5 transmission.

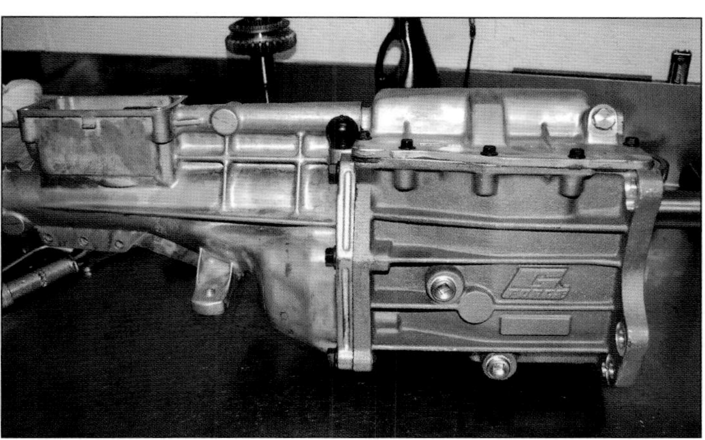

JT5 Enduro gear set with modular countergear and removable dog rings.

Here is a JT5 Enduro transmission built with G-Force's new heavy-duty T5 case. You can get this case in standard Ford Toploader, GM, and Ford T5 bolt patterns.

G-Force makes cast-bronze and billet-machined shift forks for the T5. This transmission has a JT5 Enduro gearset loaded in a G-Force case.

Chrysler A833 4-Speed Transmission

Chrysler formed a manufacturing alliance with New Process in 1964, and from this alliance the A833 4-speed was created. Over the years, the transmission evolved, but it provided reliable and efficient performance until its discontinuance in 1979. The fully synchronized transmission was offered in most Chrysler cars, such as for A-, B-, C-, E-bodied cars from 1964 until the mid-1970s. During this time, the A833 established a reputation for outstanding performance and reliability.

A tail-mounted shifter and retangular 10-bolt side cover clearly distinguishes the A833 transmission from many other manual transmissions. The A833 is a side-loaded transmission with all gears situated in the main case. In addition, the A833 has a 7⅜-inch bell housing, and its internals are different than other gearboxes. By comparison, the T10 and Muncie 4-speeds use a reverse gearset outboard of the main case. The outboard design requires an additional mid plate. Use of the additional mid section can create stability and alignment issues. The A833 not only eliminated the mid section, but it added a larger center-to-center distance to the gearset. The T10 and Muncie had 3.25-inch center-to-centers. The A833 was elongated to 3.375 inches, and the A833 became the strongest 4-speed in its class. Not much time passed before people began adapting this transmission to other makes.

From 1975 on, Chrysler released an A833 with an overdrive gear for its range of manual-transmission-equipped vehicles. The New Process overdrive 4-speed was installed on cars, such as the 225 Slant Six Duster, for improved fuel efficiency. In the older four-speed gearbox, fourth gear

New Process built the 18-spline (above) and the 23-spline (below) input shafts for 1964-1972 A833 transmissions. The 18-spline shafts were used for the 426 Wedge, 426 Hemi and 440 while the 23-spline shafts were used for 361, 383, 400, and other Mopar engines.

had a 1:1 ratio, the new gearbox's third gear became .73:1 for overdrive, and the forth gear remained 1:1 direct drive. The 3-4 shift lever was turned over to accommodate this new gearset arrangement.

Input shafts came with 23 or 18 splines. Output shafts in early versions had 23, 26, or 30 splines. Only 18-spline inputs came with 30-spline outputs. These were typically dubbed "Hemi" boxes. The 18-spline unit was used with 426 Wedge, 426 Hemi and 440 while the 23-spline shafts were used for 361, 383, 400, and other engines. As a note, if you want to swap the input shafts or gearsets, you can use the bearing retainer and front input bearing, which definitely saves times. It was easy to swap in an A833 for automatic-equipped Mopars and hence became a common procedure for muscle car owners.

These transmissions are cast-iron and very stout, and it is very important that you understand that these transmissions are extremely heavy. The A833 built through the 1960s and early 1970s were cast-iron; aluminum cases were introduced in the mid 1970s. These cast-iron units can weigh more than 115 pounds—a heavy transmission, such as this, if not supported correctly can break your fingers if it rolls onto them.

Chrysler's New Process Gear manufactured the A833. It was also the only transmission ever offered from the factory with slick-shifted gears. Besides incorporating the slick-shift process, race Hemi-style transmissions came with better alloy gears and bronze bushed speed gears to reduce frictional losses as well as gear-to-mainshaft seizures.

New Process Gear once touted itself as "The Largest Gear Manufacturer in the World." Located slightly

These are variations of the A833 case. Note the different extension housings and bearing bores.

Typical bushed race gear. Notice the paint marking, used to identify the type of gear.

Here is a Hemi countergear with purple paint. Also notice the machined grooves for identification and assembly purposes.

The Super T10 4-speed first gear on the left isn't really "super" compared to the larger Hemi first gear on the right.

Here is a factory race Hemi input with factory slick-shifted engagement teeth.

A twisted Hemi input shaft. These are extremely heavy-duty shafts that require enormous abuse to bend. However, where there is a will, there is a way!

A 1-2 slick-shift slider with a speed gear inside it shows how the overall shift gap is increased.

Passon Performance cast every tail combination in high-strength aluminum alloy.

These are original cases. Notice that the factory alloy case was beefed up to handle the remaining weight of the unit.

north of the city center of Syracuse, New York, this large manufacturing plant has now been converted to modernly appointed loft apartments. Interestingly, the company's water tower still stands, rusting away, in the middle of it all.

A company called Passon Performance has reproduced just about every part of the A833 transmission, which has been a major undertaking because so many variations exist. Popular race sets are available. For weight savings, all case configurations have been meticulously reproduced in aluminum—an iron A833 can tip the scales at 125 pounds.

Chrysler A833 Transmission Ratios

1964–1975 Chrysler A833

First	Second	Third	Fourth	Reverse	Engine Size
3.09	1.92	1.39	1.00	3.00	225/273/318
2.81	1.93	1.39	1.00	2.57	426/440
2.59	1.77	1.34	1.00	2.36	426/440
2.65	1.61	1.39	1.00	2.57	426/440
2.65	1.93	1.39	1.00	2.81	8 Cylinder, except above
2.44	1.77	1.34	1.00	2.40	8 Cylinder, except above

1964–1975 Chrysler A833 Race

First	Second	Third	Fourth	Reverse	Color Code/Engine
2.65	1.80	1.39	1.00	2.73	426/440
2.65	1.64	1.29	1.00	2.73	Green Stripe
2.14	1.43	1.19	1.00	N/A	Yellow Stripe
2.65	1.93	1.39	1.00	2.81	White Stripe
2.65	1.64	1.19	1.00	N/A	Red Stripe
2.65	1.57	1.29	1.00	N/A	Blue Stripe
2.65	1.75	1.19	1.00	N/A	Purple Stripe

1975–1980 Chrysler A833 Overdrive

First	Second	Third	Fourth	Reverse	Engine Size
3.09	1.67	1.00	.74	3.00	225/318
3.09	1.67	1.00	.72	3.00	225/318

General Motors also used aluminum and iron versions of the A833 from 1981 to1985. Many parts from these versions interchange with older units. Typically found in GMC Sierra pickups, the A833 was renamed the NP440 and has been a popular 4-speed conversion for GM muscle cars because it has the same bolt pattern and splines as a Muncie 4-speed.

Step-by-step procedures and general parameters for rebuilding the A833 is covered here, but keep in mind, there are several variations in bearing combinations as well as types of side covers. Therefore, there may be some variation in the rebuilding procedures depending on the A833 you're rebuilding.

For the most part, you can reverse the disassembly of the transmission to put it together. I've included some techniques that may help you make assembly a little easier. Installation of bushings, seals, and needle bearings have already been covered.

Disassembly

1 Remove Side Cover

Use a ratchet and socket to remove the 12 bolts that secure the side cover to the case. Take note of where each bolt comes from, because some units have different length bolts for certain positions. Fish out the forks and check them for wear.

Special Tool

2 Remove Front Bearing Retainer

Remove the 4 bolts that hold the front bearing retainer. Use a snap-ring pliers to expand and remove the snap ring that locates the input shaft to the front bearing. My method for disassembly is based on the fact that most people do not have a special front bearing puller.

3 Remove Speedometer Gear

Use a ratchet and socket or (as shown) a drill with a socket and extension to remove the bolt and hold-down for the speedometer gear. Take note of the location of the fitting, so you can easily install it when the time comes.

Important!

4 Align Speedometer Gear

The A833 uses an offset speedometer fitting for the speedo driven gear. The numbers correspond to the range of tooth counts for the gear. The raised index mark on the gear lines up with an alignment mark on the extension housing. You must reinstall this fitting in the correct position. If it is reinstalled in the wrong position, your speedometer will not to work or it will strip the gear.

5 Remove Extension Housing Bolts

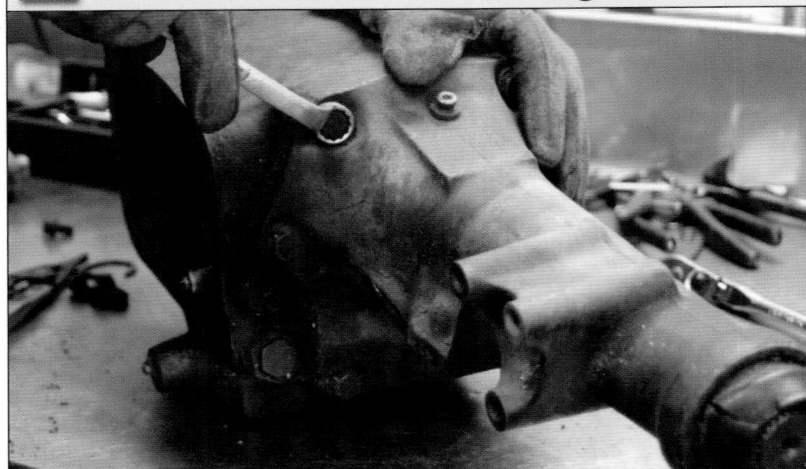

Unlike the Muncies and T10s, this extension actually holds the complete gear assembly. This design eliminates the mid plate bearing support and the extra parting line, so a stronger case is effectively built. It will not pull out, so don't try to force it.

6 Remove Countershaft

Pry on the extension housing with an old screwdriver just enough to break it free. Rotate it 180 degrees, so the countershaft is exposed. This allows you to remove it and drop the countergear out of the way of the upper geartrain.

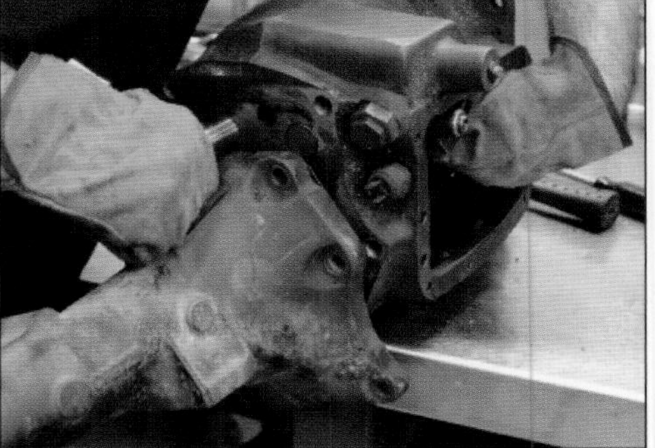

Once you start removing the countershaft, support the countergear with your other hand to take pressure off the shaft. This helps it come out. These components are really heavy, so use work gloves rather than thin surgical gloves to protect your hands. There is a small woodruff key that will come out.

7 Remove the Extension and Geartrain

With the countergear dropped, you can remove the extension and geartrain assembly.

8 Drive Input Shaft into Case

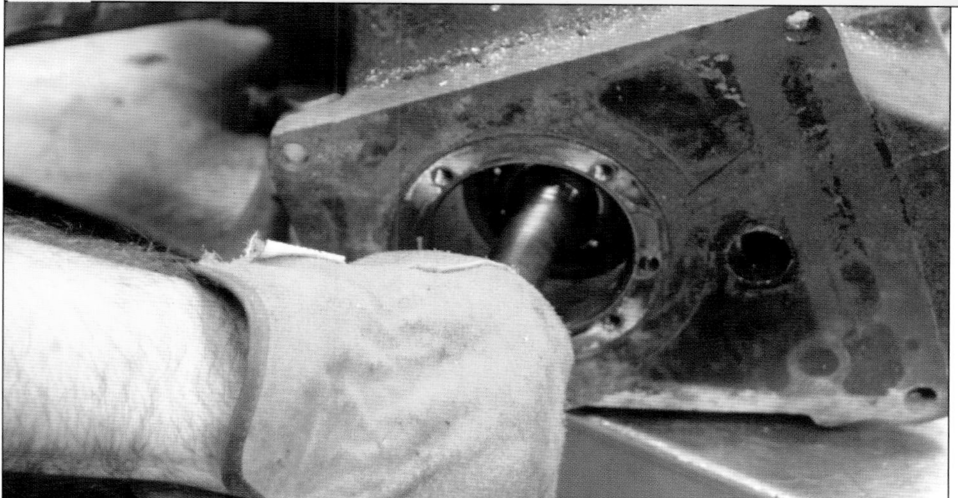

Use snap-ring pliers to remove the front bearing's outer retaining snap ring and use a mallet to carefully tap the input shaft with the bearing through the case. Units that have the larger-style bearing are not able to use this technique. Instead keep the bearing supported by the outer ring on the case and press the input shaft of the bearing using the case as a support.

9 Remove Countergear

Now you have a clean shot at removing the countergear. If you're going to reuse the needles, you may want to do this over some sort of tray to avoid losing any. However, in many cases, it's a good idea to replace the needles, especially if it is a higher-mileage transmission that is being rebuilt.

Broken Shifter Shaft

This unit has a broken reverse shifter shaft. It is quite common for these to strip and break because they have a very small 5/16-inch coarse thread. The reverse light switch is located here as well as the reverse detent fitting assembly.

10 Remove Detent Assembly

I've removed the complete reverse detent assembly and reverse switch. These simply unscrew from the main case. Don't bother trying to take the upper part of the detent assembly apart because it's easier to do that off the transmission and supported firmly in a vice. A 3/8-inch detent ball and spring will fall out.

11 Remove Reverse Idler Shaft

Punch out the reverse idler shaft. Sometimes a long punch or an offset pry bar will work when going in from the front of the case. This shaft also has a woodruff key. Notice the slot for it.

12 Remove Reverse Idler Gear and Parts

Once the idler shaft has been removed, you can remove the reverse idler gear, reverse fork, and shifter shaft.

13 Disengage Rear Bearing Retaining Ring

Start disassembling the upper geartrain by squeezing the rear bearing retaining ring ends together. You can use a regular set of adjustable pliers to do this. Move it forward to dislodge the retaining ring from the groove in the extension housing.

14 Remove Output Shaft

Sometimes the bearing gets stuck in the bore, so gently tap the output shaft with a hammer to start removal. Be careful not to overdo it and damage the shaft.

As the whole output shaft assembly comes out of the tail, make sure you don't knock off the 3-4 synchro hub. Some of the synchro strut keys are not readily available parts, so you don't want to lose any of these keys.

15 Remove 3-4 Synchro and Third Gear

Use a snap-ring pliers to remove the snap ring that secures the 3-4 synchro assembly and third gear to the mainshaft. Once the snap ring has been removed, the 3-4 synchro assembly and third gear slide off the mainshaft.

Documentation Required

16 Note Position of 3-4 Assembly

Once the 3-4 assembly has been removed, take note of the position of the slider because it needs to be assembled in the same position. The A833 later-style rings have the indexing dog built into the ring. This reduces side load on the strut key.

17 Remove Rear Bearing Snap Ring

Notice that the speedometer drive gear is actually part of the main shaft. This is a great design feature simply because you never have to pull the transmission apart for a speedometer gear failure.

18 Press Off Rear Bearing

Support the assembly under first gear. You can use a press or just tap the output shaft to press off the rear bearing. An old Muncie case is used to support the main shaft, so the work can be performed.

19 Remove First Gear Synchro Ring

Once the rear bearing has been pressed off, the first gear and first-gear synchro ring simply slide off the mainshaft.

20 Remove 1-2 Synchro Snap Ring

Use a snap-ring pliers to remove the 1-2 synchro snap ring. The complete 1-2 assembly, second-gear synchro ring, and second gear lift off the shaft once the snap ring has been removed.

21 Press Off Input Shaft Bearing

Press off the input shaft bearing using a shop press. This image shows the smaller 307-style bearing. Other units have the larger 308SG8 bearing.

Bearing Styles

These are the two style bearings of the A833. Units can have two small- or two large-style bearings or a combination of small and large.

Synchro Assembly Parts

The hubs and sliders of both synchro assemblies are laid out, so you can see the correct order of these parts. The right side of the picture would be the rear of the transmission. Note that the hubs are offset toward the front. Notice that the 1-2 hub has a longer offset than the 3-4 hub. For complete synchro ring assembly instructions, refer to page 26.

The ring on the left is the later style that has a built-in dog; the early style is shown on the right. These rings use different strut keys and synchronizer assemblies. Because the transmissions are so old, it is not uncommon to see a mix of early and later assemblies in an A833.

22 Install Side Cover

This side cover uses a comb detent and interlock system as on a Muncie 4-speed. I've chosen to use this cover in the buildup, but it is more difficult of the two styles to install.

Interlock System

This side cover uses a sprung-ball type of interlock similar to the ones used in all T10-style transmissions.

Professional Mechanic Tip

23 Shift Fork Ends

This image illustrates the two basic style shift fork ends. The fork on the left is iron and is used with the comb-style cover. The bronze fork on the right is used in the ball detent cover. I actually used an iron 3-4 T10 shift fork as a replacement for the bronze 3-4 fork. You simply space it in with hardened washers.

24 Inspect Shifter Shaft

This shifter shaft shows wear at the end. If the linkage arm does not fit tight on the rectangular tab, it will always work loose. After inspecting the shafts, deburr the ends and replace the O-rings.

25 Disassemble Reverse Detent

Secure the reverse detent in a vise and use a ratchet and socket to disassemble it.

Order of Countergear Bearings and Spacers

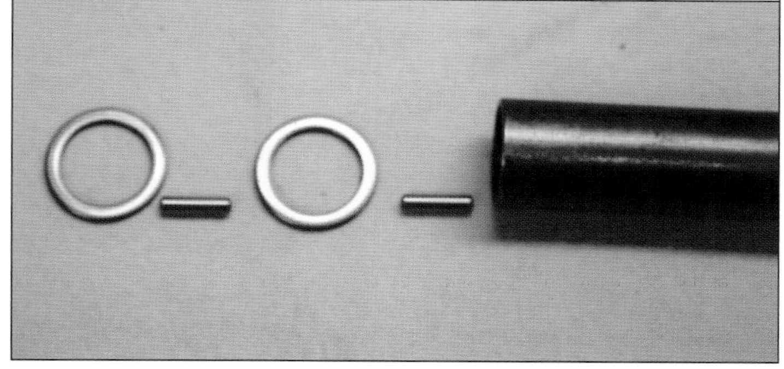

This is how the countergear needle bearings and spacers stack. Use assembly gel to hold the needles inside the gear.

26 Inspect Reverse Gear

This design, which incorporates the reverse gear as part of the countergear, has at least one disadvantage. If the reverse section is damaged, you need to replace the entire countergear because reverse is a non-synchronized gear. After inspecting this gearing, we found out that it is still useable.

Assembly

1 Insert Strut Keys in Hub

Use assembly gel to hold the strut keys in place in the hub. The later style can fall out of the hub if you move the slider to far.

2 Align Synchro Ring with Slider

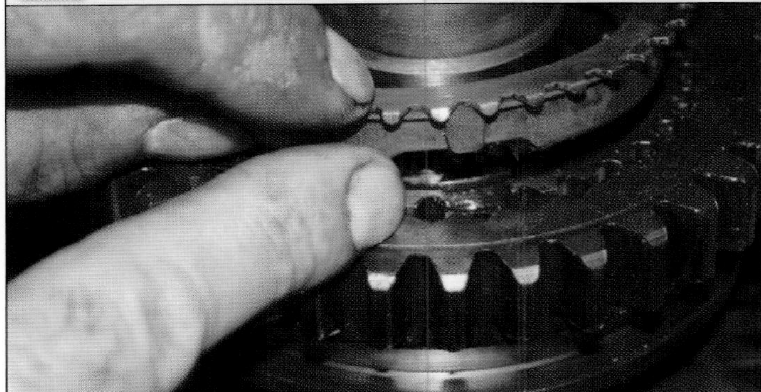

You need to catch the later-style synchro ring's dog section in the key slot of the slider and hold the ring in place with assembly gel.

3 Install Retaining Ring on Mainshaft

Remember to place the rear bearing retaining ring on the mainshaft before reinstalling a new rear bearing. It's a lot easier to install it now than later in the process.

4 Install Rear Bearing in Extension Housing

Support the output assembly in a vise. Always clean the rear housing bearing bore with emery cloth and then spray WD-40 in it, so the extension housing slides back onto the rear bearing much easier. You must compress the snap-ring tabs together to work it back into place.

5 Seat Rear Bearing Retaining Ring

Use a small screwdriver to make sure the rear bearing retaining ring is fully seated in the extension housing.

6 Install Fork, Idler Gear and Idler Shaft

Install a new O-ring on the reverse shifter shaft. In addition, install the fork, idler gear, and idler shaft. The fork groove of the idler gear faces toward the rear. Notice that I have installed the detent sleeve but have not fully assembled the rest of it.

7 Install New Needle Bearings Inside the Input Shaft

As seen in other transmission rebuilds in this book, use assembly grease to hold the needle bearing inside the input shaft. Place the input shaft on the front of the output shaft and push the 3-4 slider forward to keep them together. Notice the position of the keys and slider. Pushing the slider too far will cause the keys to fly out, so be extra careful.

Torque Fasteners

8 Install Upper Geartrain

Now that the counter gear has been placed back in the case, we are ready to install the upper geartrain. I tend to favor gluing the gasket on the main case to make it stay in place during assembly. This is my basic angle of approach to get the whole upper geartrain back in place. Once the extension is installed, I bolt it in place. Torque the rear bolts to 40 ft-lbs.

Torque Fasteners

9 Install Front Bearing

To install the front bearing, hold and pull the input shaft outward while using a punch to tap the bearing into place. Work the bearing down, side to side. Once seated, install both the outside locating snap ring and the inside rings with a snap-ring pliers. Install the front bearing retainer with a new seal and gasket. Torque the four front bearing retainer bolts to 20 ft-lbs.

10 Install Shifter Forks and Shafts

The 1-2 shift fork must be correctly positioned on the 1-2 slider. Install both forks, along with their corresponding shifter shafts, in the case when working with a comb-style cover. Use plenty of assembly gel to hold all the parts in place.

Important!

Use plenty of gel or grease on the shifter shafts. Locate the shafts on the cover and wiggle it down into place. Be careful not to cut up the O-rings and do not force or hammer it!

Torque Fasteners

11 Install Side Cover Over Detent Combs

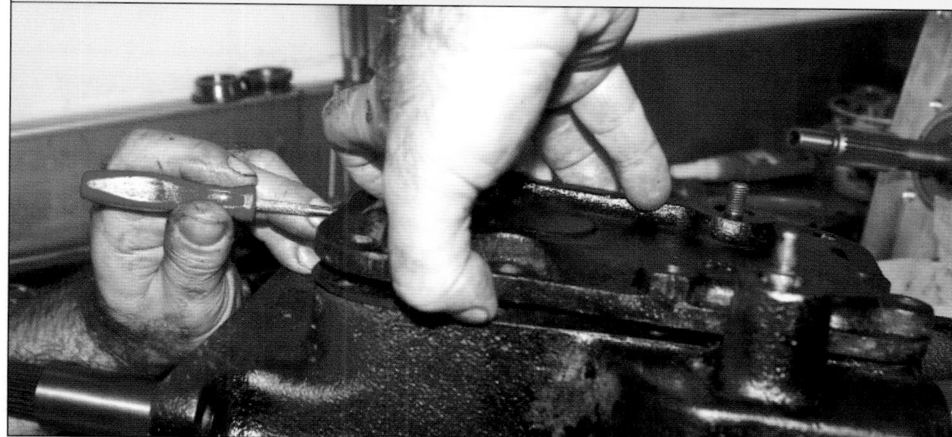

The cover drops down and stops when the ends of the forks butt up against the detent combs. You usually have about a 3/8-inch gap at this point. Use a small screwdriver to push the comb ends over the forks, which allows the cover to drop into place. If this were a ball-style detent cover, you would simply install the shift forks and drop the cover assembly down onto the forks. Torque the cover bolts to 20 ft-lbs.

12 Install Reverse Detent Ball and Parts

Install the reverse detent ball, spring, detent end cap, and the reverse light switch. The factory had little paper gaskets for these parts, which are not easily available. The 51813 gasket eliminator works well.

13 Install Speedometer Gear

This is a 32-tooth speedometer gear. Rotate the 32-38 index mark until it aligns with the mark on the tail. Then install the hold-down and bolt.

The A833 has been completely rebuilt. Typically, Dextron II or Dextron III lubricant is used in the A833. That's what was in this box and that is what I will use to refill it.

GM/MUNCIE 4-SPEED TRANSMISSIONS

The Muncie 4-speed was GM's answer to the T10, and by mid 1962 full working prototypes had been built. It replaced the T10 in General Motors' cars, starting in February of 1963. Corvettes saw installation by May through June of 1963. It was based on the T10 design, and I have been told that BorgWarner engineers helped design it. In fact, first- and second-speed gears were identical in tooth count and pitch. Some of the later versions of the T10 had 9310 Nickel alloy gears. Because the first-speed gears were identical to the Muncie except for internal bore and synchro cone sizes, a company called Stahl made an adapter sleeve to be able to use the stronger T10 first gear in the Muncie. The first Muncie in 1963 had a "thin fin" tail-housing and a 6207-style bearing in the front. First gear rode directly on the mainshaft. By 1964, first gear rode on a sleeved bushing, the front bearing diameter was increased, and the webbing on the tailhousing was increased.

As power levels climbed in 1965 and GM started putting big-block engines in cars, the countershaft diameter increased from 7/8 to 1 inch by 1966. The Muncie had several ratios, case configurations, and spline counts. The last year GM offered the Muncie was 1974. However, some early 1975 cars built in 1974 had Muncies. The Super T10, an improved version of the T10, was reintroduced in 1975 GM cars. Power levels dropped in 1975, requiring different gearing. Since the ST10 had better ratio options, it probably was cheaper for GM to purchase complete transmissions rather than tool up to make different gears for the Muncie.

How to Identify a Muncie

People commonly call a Muncie an M21. Or they think a Muncie passenger-car transmission is the same as a Muncie truck transmission. They are not. What do M20, M21, and M22 actually mean? The "M" codes are RPO (Regular Production Option) codes. They don't mean Muncie. You can have an M21 4-speed in a 1979 Camaro, and it is actually a close-ratio Super T10.

To correctly identify a Muncie, you need three things: First, you need a main case casting number. Second, you need a spline count of both input and output shafts and confirmation of any rings or grooves existing around the input shaft splines. Third, you need the date codes and VIN numbers that help confirm that the case and gears belong together. Tooth counts on the input shaft help confirm a certain gear ratio. However, you may not have access to this information if the transmission is still in the car, or a vendor at a swap meet is unwilling to remove the cover. Sometimes replacement inputs have no ID grooves.

All 26-spline inputs came with 32-spline output shafts and all 10-spline inputs came with 27-spline output shafts. A common mistake is thinking that all "fine spline" 26-spline input shafts are M22 heavy-duty types. This is not true. An M22 gearbox has about a 20-degree helix angle on the gearset, rather than a 37-degree angle.

Also, M22 gearsets were made of a different heat-treated alloy. The straighter angle was designed to produce less end loading of the geartrain

RPO M Code Examples

Model	Type
MC1	Transmission; 3-speed
M11	Shift Lever; floor mounted
M20	Transmission; 4-speed wide-ratio
M21	Transmission; 4-speed close-ratio
M22	Transmission; 4-speed close-ratio heavy-duty
M35	Transmission; Powerglide automatic with 6-cyl
M39	Transmission; 5-speed BorgWarner
M40	Transmission; Turbo Hydra-Matic automatic with 6-cyl

and less heat, but it created more noise, thus the nickname "Rock-crusher." The heat-treated/shotpeen process allowed for more impact of the gears.

If the Muncie has a drain plug, it does not necessarily identify it as an M22. Again, the first M22 boxes had drain plugs, but all 3925661 castings had drain plugs. And by 1969, most Muncies had drain plugs.

Serial and VIN Numbers

Serial numbers for Muncie 4-speeds always begin with the letter "P," which stands for Muncie plant. (Because the Muncie 3-speed used the M-designator, the letter P was used to identify 4-speed transmissions assembled in the Muncie plant). P does not mean passenger car. If P stood for passenger car, you'd see it stamped on every 4-speed, including a T10, but you don't.

The serial number tells you the date the transmission was built in a particular production year. Serial numbers from 1963 to 1966 included only the month and day. For example, P0102 indicates that the Muncie was built on January 2. From 1967 to1968, the serial number began with a number designator for the year, and then a letter designator for the month. For example, P8A01 means January 1, 1968.

One important point: A Muncie dated with a December build date was actually built the prior year. An example would be P8T13—8 is for a 1968 production car, "T" stands for December, and 13 is the day. It was actually built in December of 1967 for the 1968 model year. To confirm this, simply look at the VIN number; it usually has a lower production sequence, justifying an early build.

The 1969 to 1974 Muncies got a ratio designator added to the end of the serial number. An example would be P4D23B. This equates to April 23, 1974, M21 ratio.

Putting It All Together

Start by looking at the main-case casting number. Using the charts, you can determine the date range that a particular casting was used. Check to see if the input shaft has any rings around the splines and then check the stamped P code to help determine ratio.

VIN numbers can help you confirm year, model, and make as well. Later VINs have assembly plant codes and years. For example, a VIN starting with 19N is a 1969 Chevrolet made in the Norwood plant, while one starting with 29N is a 1969 Pontiac made in the Norwood plant. This could be useful for finding out what car the transmission was originally in. However, I always say GM never designed this system for people to accurately decipher codes 40-plus years later at a swap meet. You can be sure that in those years a great number of transmissions have been assembled out of spare parts and cannibalized. So I always like to pull the cover, look at the gears, and count teeth to verify what I think I have.

Some input shafts produced by the aftermarket and General Motors have no identifying rings on them. The rings originally corresponded with rings or grooves on the countergear so that the assembler matched a one- or two-ring input with a one- or two-ring countergear. When manufacturing was stopped, GM stopped making inputs with these marks, probably to save machining operations.

Unfortunately, you cannot always use the OD grooves on input shafts as a sure-fire method of identification.

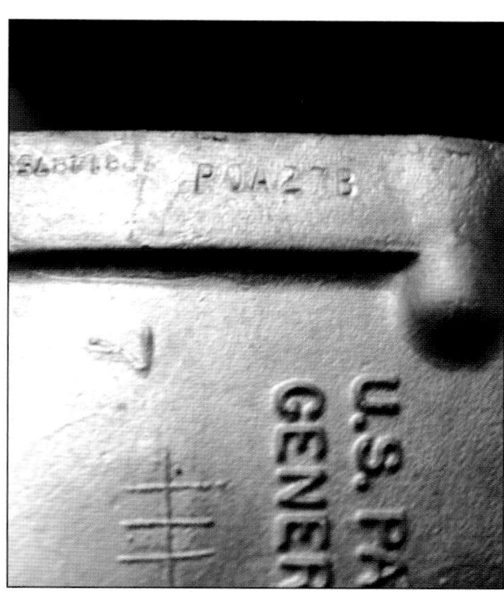

This shows the typical VIN and serial number stampings on a Muncie.

Muncie Ratio Designator

Code	Type
A	M20
B	M21
C	M22

Transmission Plant Codes

Code	Type
A	Cleveland Torquedrive
B	Cleveland THM 350
C	Cleveland Powerglide
E	McKinnon Industries Powerglide
H	Muncie HD three-speed
K	McKinnon three-speed
M	Muncie three-speed
P	Muncie four-speed
R	Saginaw four-speed
S	Saginaw three-speed
T	Toledo Powerglide
Y	Toledo THM 350

Month Codes (1967–1974)

Code	Month
A	January
B	February
C	March
D	April
E	May
H	June
K	July
M	August
P	September
R	October
S	November
T	December

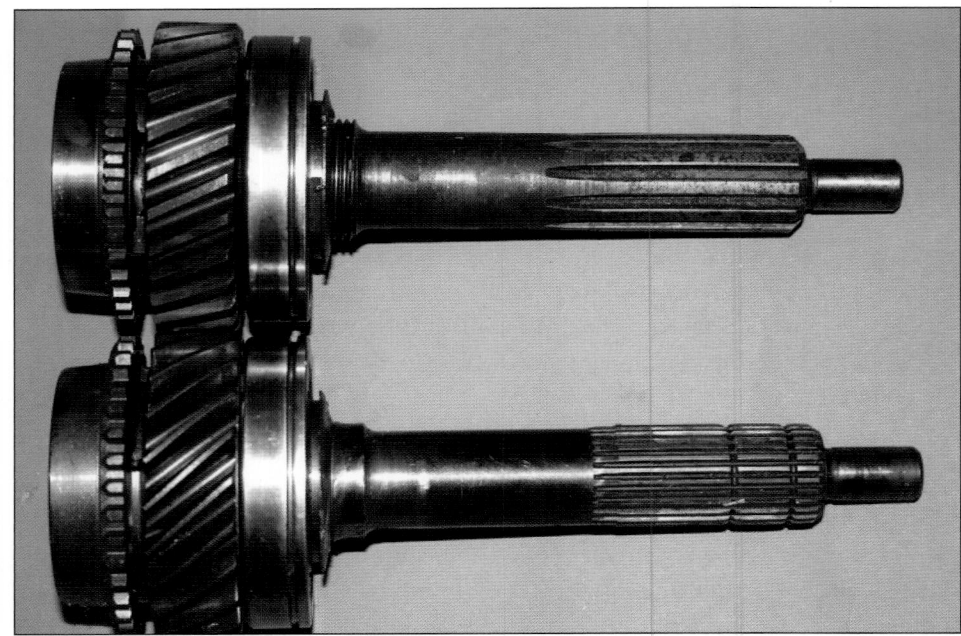

The top gear is a 10-spline M22; the bottom gear is a 26-spline M20. Note the two grooves on the input designating the M20 ratio.

These GM gears are both 10-spline M20 inputs; however, only the bottom one has OD grooves.

M22 Rockcrushers and the New Muncies

Alan Colvin, author of *Chevrolet by Numbers,* and Brian Higgins of SK Speed documented that 7/8-inch-diameter M22 countergears did exist. Since the 7/8-inch bore was pre-1966, it suggests that the M22 transmissions were for 1965 cars. Colvin discovered a Chevrolet Engineering Change Recommendation was issued in December 19, 1964, requiring a change of the M20/M21-style transmission to the M22 because of the Grand Sport Corvette Race Program. Prototypes

Muncie 4-Speed Case Casting Numbers

Casting ID	Year	Description
3831704	1963	Only small 6207NR front bearing, 7/8" bore
3839606	1963–1964	Regular bearing, 7/8" bore
3851325	1964–1965	7/8" bore, mostly 1964
3851325	1964–1965	7/8" bore
3864606	1965–	3864–1965, 7/8" bore, milled-off last 3 digits
3885010	1966–1967	1" bore
3925660	1968–1970	1" bore, 1970–1974 (some early 1975 cars)

Two odd castings rarely seen in Muncie 4-speeds are the 3839606 and the milled and unmilled versions of the 3864606.

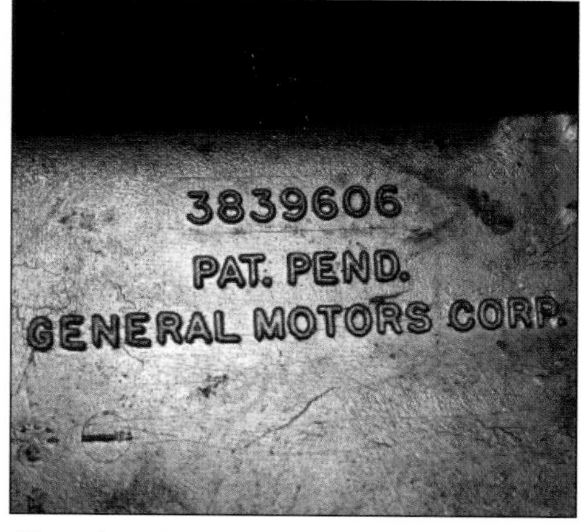

Here is a 3839606 casting, which is very rare. Sometimes odd castings like this show up that are not necessarily documented in restoration guides, but they do indeed exist!

Muncie M20, M21, M22 Ratios

Year	Type	Rings	Ratio
1963–1965	M20	None	2.56/1.91/1.48/1.00/3.16
1966–1974	M20	Two	2.52/1.88/1.46/1.00/3.11
1963–1974	M21	One	2.20/1.64/1.28/1.00/2.27
1967–1974	M22	None	2.20/1.64/1.28/1.00/2.27

This is a 1965 casting with the factory numbers milled off.

Muncie M20, M21, M22 Input Shaft Tooth and Spline Count Related to Year

Year	Type	Rings	Spline	Tooth Count
1963–1965	M20	None	10	24
1966–1970	M20	Two	10	21
1970–1974	M20	Two	26	21
1963–1970	M21	One	10	26
1970–1974	M21	One	26	26
1967–1970	M22	None	10	26
1969–1974	M22	None	26	26

had the 7/8-inch countergear, but 57 M22s were built using 3851325 cases modified with 1-inch bores and added drain plugs, and they had the casting number completely milled off. It's hard to imagine that 40-plus years later we are still designing transmissions based on the M22 concept.

I've always said the M22 was not a drag-race but a road-race transmission. Yet drag racing was much more popular in the 1960s than road racing. Today, we either have helical gears or straight-cut spur gears. Think of the M22 gears as semi-helical. The low helix angle of M22 gears produces less heat, less side loading, and stronger load distribution across the gear tooth. It more efficiently transmits power than a spur gearset, and it is not as noisy. The whine of the M22 gearset is a characteristic of that low helix angle. Four decades ago, we could run street cars with a 4.56 axle ratio, but today this is rarely done. These came with a 2.20 first-gear ratio, and this "dead" ratio just doesn't work well today. That is why newer 5-speeds are all the rage.

GM Speedometer Ratios

With so many different tire sizes and axle ratios available today, it is not unusual to be driving around with an inaccurate speedometer. Since speedometer gearsets varied among makes and models, and the same model could have different axle codes, it was not uncommon for the same Muncie 4-speed to have several unique part numbers based on different speedometer gearsets.

Someone may ask: "Do you know what speedometer gears I would need for my 1967 GTO with a 3.55 rear?" Most don't know their tire diameter or don't realize that changing axle ratios and tire sizes changes the speedometer reading. This is a weekly question for me, so I thought the following quick-reference may help.

The speedometer drive gear (the one that goes on the mainshaft) commonly comes with either a 7- or 8-tooth worm gear. You determine the number of worm teeth by laying the gear on its side and counting each tooth as it comes to an end. They come in two outside diameters (1.76 and 1.84 inches) as well as two inside diameters to coincide with 27- and 32-spline output shafts. Units built in 1969 and 1970 had plastic versions of the 8-tooth 1.84-inch-diameter gear, which is held on with a clip. Always replace these with a press-on steel gear. The factory only used 8-tooth 1.84-inch-diameter gears on the 32-spline shafts, but you can also get 7-tooth ones from the aftermarket. There is an early 6-tooth drive gear, which is not available for the driven pencil gear, so I always recommend getting rid of them.

Calculating Speedometer Errors

You can download equations from the Internet to determine your correct speedometer reading at a given speed with a certain tire size and axle ratio. GM vehicles that use the Muncie and T10 can make use of the equation below:

$$\text{Speedometer Gear Ratio (SGR)} = (63{,}360 \times \text{Axle Ratio}) \div (3{,}141.6 \times \text{Tire Diameter})$$

So, if the vehicle has a 3.08 rear axle and 26-inch tires, your SGR ratio equals 2.389.

To determine the driven gear's tooth count, multiply the number of teeth on the mainshaft drive gear by the SGR.

$$\text{Tooth Count} = \text{Number of Mainshaft Teeth} \times \text{SGR}$$

If you have an 8-tooth drive gear, your driven gear is a 19-tooth.

Here's another method, which works for any make or model, that's pretty accurate. This is particularly useful for fixing errors when changing out rear-axle ratios, yet it retains the same tire size from the factory. The above example has a car with a 3.08 rear, 19-tooth driven gear and 8-tooth drive gear. These gears form a speedometer factor (SF). The formula to find it is:

$$\text{Speedometer Factor} = (\text{Drive Gear} \div \text{Driven Gear}) \times \text{Axle Ratio}$$

Use the same gears and axle ratio and you come up with an SF of 1.296:1.

Now you have changed the axle ratio to 3.55:1. Because you know what the original SF was and your drive gear is fixed, you can find the new driven gear count by using the following formula:

$$\text{New Driven Gear Tooth Count} = (\text{Drive Gear} \times \text{Axle Ratio}) \div \text{SF}$$

Using the above formula, you now have to replace the 19-tooth gear with a 22-tooth gear as per your calculation.

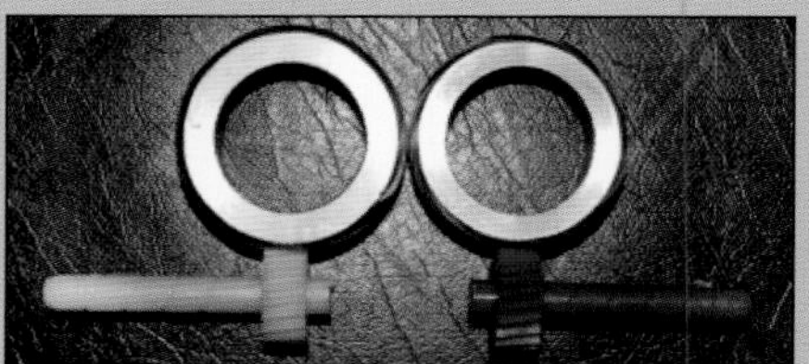

The larger-diameter steel gear (top) uses a smaller driven "pencil" gear. The smaller steel gear (bottom) uses a larger-diameter driven gear. Use the wrong combination, and you'll either have no speedometer reading because the gears are not meshing or the gears are stripping!

By 2000, almost every Muncie 4-speed that came into the shop had badly worn gears because the main case was either worn or repaired. George Sollish, president of Auto Gear Company, asked me about building a new Muncie 4-speed case and what improvements needed to be made. Using input from myself and several other volume rebuilders, he designed the Muncie Supercase. The case had thicker mounting ears with improved webbing, used a wider sealed front bearing, and incorporated soft plug sealing on the countershaft. This addressed ear breakage problems and leakage issues. The case casting uses state-of-the-art techniques that yield less-stress risers combined with a better heat-treated aluminum. Gradually, more and more new components were added. I suggested a nodular iron mid plate, and the Superplate was created. A new side cover followed and then new tailhousings. One of the parameters was to make every part backward compatible, so you could bolt-up any older Muncie parts to the new stuff.

By May 2003, we were building complete new Muncie-style transmissions with all-new components. Specialty gear ratios were created to give the Muncie a modern street approach as well as make it more competitive on the race track. You can now get an M22 with a 2.56 first gear or an extra-close-ratio M22X with a 1.17 third-gear ratio. There are also overdrive conversion gearsets. See the Muncie build up in this chapter—a great deal of the recently designed parts are used in the build.

Muncie 4-Speed Rebuild

The transmission for this rebuild had quite a few of the common problems associated with 40-year-old transmissions. This Muncie was of the early 1964–1965 era. Because of the age and condition of this transmission, it became a candidate for some of the newer-style upgrades.

Muncies really don't need to have any measurements taken. If something is worn, replace it. Parts are cheap enough. Countergear endplay should be no more than 0.035 inch. If your endplay is excessive, then you have wear on the countergear thrust surface or maincase. You can compensate for wear by making shims out of shim stock to bring the thrust washers more in spec. I still prefer new parts.

Disassembly

1 Start Disassembly

This transmission looks fine from the outside, but do not take things at face value.

2 Note Damaged Countershaft Hole

A closer look reveals a stretched-out countershaft hole, which was hand peened with a punch to try to make the loose shaft fit tighter. That is not the correct way to repair this problem.

3 Slide Cover Interlock Support Pin

The side cover interlock support pin (between the two shifter shafts) is an early design, which can fall inside the transmission during use. Newer styles have an outside support flange.

4 Punch Out the Lock Pin

Use a punch and a hammer to drive the tapered lock pin for the reverse shifter shaft out from the bottom upward. If the pin is frozen, use some heat.

Documentation Required

5 Remove Side Cover

Shift the transmission into second gear, remove the seven side cover bolts, and remove the side cover. Don't worry about the shift fork or shifter shafts coming out of the cover. If you are going to reuse them, make a note as to their positions.

6 Inspect Input Shaft

A close look at the input shaft and mating countergear section, also known as the head set, reveals major breakage.

7 Pry Off Retainer

Remove the four bearing retainer bolts and pry off the retainer. Lots of transmissions have stripped threads in this section or oversized bolts and threads.

Critical Inspection

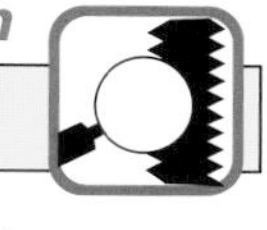

8 Inspect Front Bearing

The front bearing "gland" nut is on backward, which is a common mistake. Also note the cracked bearing. Lack of a pilot bushing or severe misalignment of the transmission and engine crankshaft usually causes the outer bearing race to crack.

9 Remove Front Bearing Nut

Always chisel off the old nut and replace them with new nuts that are in the rebuild kits. After 40 years or so, they usually seize in place and are difficult to save anyway.

10 Pry Off Front Bearing

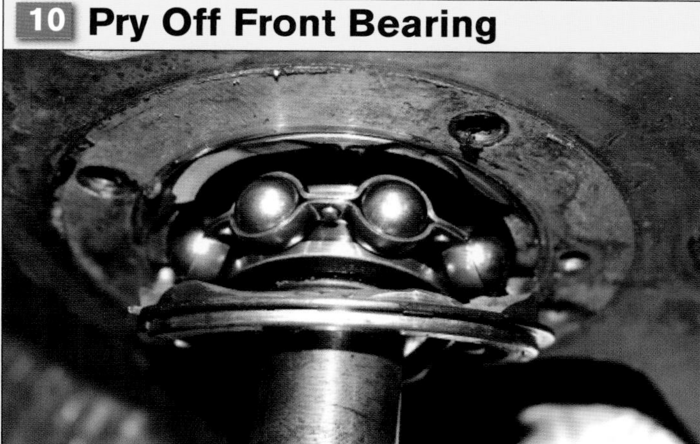

Normally, you can pry on either side of the bearing to remove it. However, badly damaged bearings like this one come out in pieces.

11 Remove Reverse Shifter Shaft

Pull out the reverse shifter shaft to disengage the reverse shift fork from the reverse gear. That's what removing the tapered pin allows you to do. Remove the six tailhousing bolts and pry off the tailhousing.

12 Remove Reverse Gear Parts

Remove the rear reverse idler gear, thrust washer, and idler shaft. Sometimes the shaft sticks in the tail. Notice that the lower reverse gear is a little rounded off from grinding in reverse.

13 Remove Output Shaft and Upper Gearset

Remove the output shaft and upper gearset from the main case. Sometimes you have to pry between the main case and the mid plate. Don't worry about things flying apart.

14 Remove Input Shaft

Pick out as many loose parts as possible, and then remove the input shaft. Broken inputs, such as this one, make great clutch-alignment tools.

Important!

15 Remove Reverse Idler and Thrust Washer

Remove forward or inside reverse idler and thrust washer. If you are reusing any thrust washers, make sure that the washer tangs are still able to prevent it from spinning.

Critical Inspection

16 Inspect Reverse Idler Gear

Inspect the forward edge of the inside reverse idler. The groove cut into the forward edge is due to the 1-2 slider hitting it. This causes a whirring noise heard only in first gear. Worn forks and slider grooves can aggravate this common design flaw.

Critical Inspection, Special Tool, Performance Tip

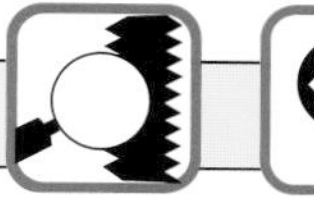

17 Fix Countershaft Bore

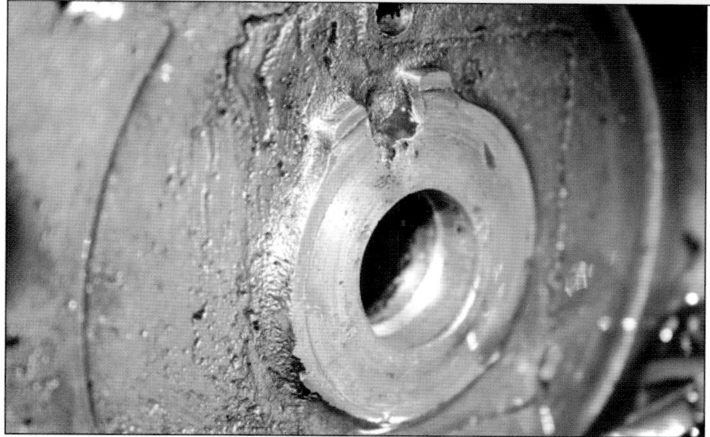

The front countershaft bore of the main case reveals a severe elongation. Boring it and installing a bushing is a common fix. This needs to be done in a machine shop on a vertical mill. Since this is a 7/8-inch-diameter countershaft, we can just bore the case to the 1-inch size and use a later-style head set. I'll scrap this case and use a new Auto Gear Supercase. If the countershaft bore is no longer a press fit and the shaft can slide in or out of the case by hand, the case needs to be repaired or replaced.

18 Update Input Shaft

The newer-style M20 input (left) has 21 teeth on a larger diameter, in contrast to 24 teeth on a smaller diameter (right). This makes for thicker and stronger gear teeth, and as a result, the input shaft can transmit more torque.

Performance Tip

19 Install Updated Countergear

The M20 countergear (right) is the new design with 25 teeth, in contrast to the early 29-tooth finer pitch (left). It also takes a 1-inch countershaft. This upgrade started in 1966. The three holes in the new gear's front face are for an anti-backlash plate. Remove these plates on every M20 countergear because they have a tendency to break or loosen.

20 Disassemble Geartrain

Remove the 3-4 synchro snap ring to start disassembling the main geartrain. Remove the 3-4 hub and third gear. Some later transmissions may require this to be pressed off.

21 Disassemble Mainshaft

Here's a trick way to disassemble the mainshaft without having to pull off the speedo gear: Use a snap-ring pliers to remove the rear snap ring that holds the rear bearing to the mainshaft, and let it rest outside the groove.

22 Press Out Gear Set

Support the assembly under second gear and press the output shaft through the whole gearset in one shot.

23 Slide Off Second Gear

The second gear, the 1-2 synchro assembly, first gear and bushing, mid plate, reverse gear, and speedometer drive gear can slide off the mainshaft.

Performance Tip

24 Upgrade Synchro Rings

We will upgrade this transmission to later-style synchro rings and hubs. The later style (left) has thicker rings, but a thinner hub, as compared to the early set (right). Early non-shouldered rings tend to crack under heavy abuse.

Performance Tip

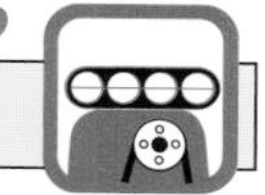

25 Inspect Mid Plate

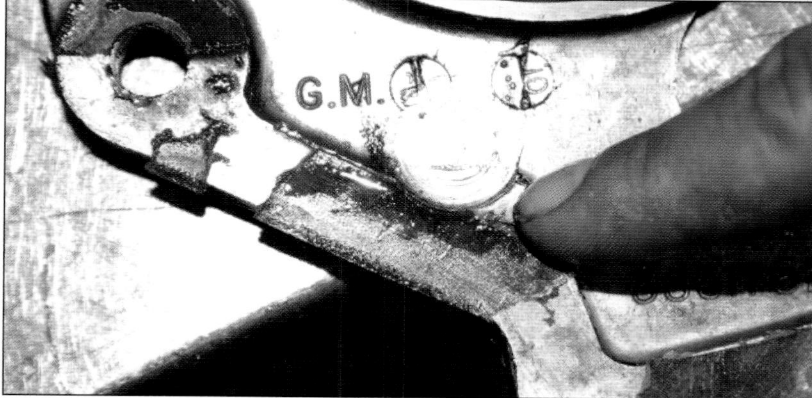

Close examination of the mid plate shows damage due to a spinning countershaft. The plate has an area to lock the pin from spinning. The plate will be upgraded to a nodular-iron Auto Gear mid plate.

26 Remove Bearing from Mid Plate

With snap-ring pliers, spread the rear bearing retaining ring open, and tap the rear bearing out of the mid plate with a punch and hammer. Most plates have snap-ring grooves that have been widened over the years. The widened grooves cause excess geartrain movement. The new nodular-iron plates fit more precisely and help "girdle" the main case as well.

Critical Inspection

27 Inspect Second and Third Gears

The second- and third-speed gears show fairly worn clutch teeth or engagement teeth. The synchro cones have permanent grooves, which may not allow new synchro rings to bite correctly. These will be replaced with new gears.

Critical Inspection

28 Inspect Front Retainer

The front bearing retainer is grooved because the nut was put on backward. This causes an air leak, which will cause an oil leak. It's time for a new retainer.

Critical Inspection

29 Inspect Shift Forks

Both shift forks show wear. When forks are worn as much as this one, shift quality can diminish. Combined with worn gears and sliders, the transmission can fall out of gear.

Damaged Parts Pile

Here is the scrap pile from this transmission so far. Hopefully, the transmission you rebuild will not be in such poor condition.

30 Remove Reverse Fork and Parts

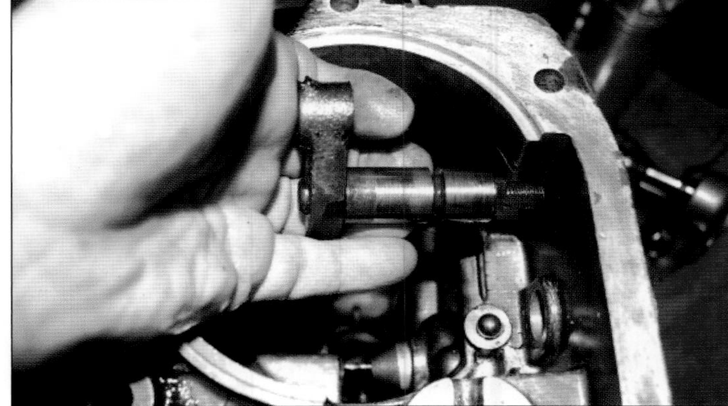

Remove the reverse fork, reverse shifter shaft, detent ball, and spring. Be careful not to lose the ball and spring.

31 Take Out Shift Shaft Seals

Use a small flathead screwdriver to remove the shift shaft seals in the side cover and tailhousing.

32 Remove Speedometer Driven Gear and Parts

Remove the speedometer driven gear, speedometer fitting, hold-down plate, and bolt from the tailhousing.

33 Remove Rear Seals

Pry out the rear seals with an old screwdriver. Most seal pullers don't work because the seals are often corroded in place. You must be careful and work the seal from side to side to remove it. Be careful because you can crack early tailhousings in the area because the castings are thin. Remove the bushing.

First-Gear Sleeves

All these gear sleeves have the center tapered in for oil collection. People look at the factory first-gear sleeve (left) and think it is worn when it is not. The rare M22 sleeve with milled flats (center) promotes better lube to first gear. The spiral shape of the oil grooves on the new Auto Gear upgrade (right) forces oil into the center of the gear.

Precision Measurement, Important!

Needle Bearing and Spacer Orientation

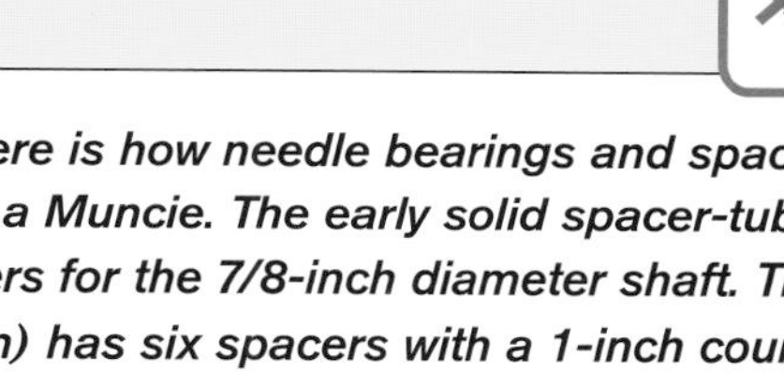

Here is how needle bearings and spacers are laid out in a Muncie. The early solid spacer-tube design (top) has four spacers for the 7/8-inch diameter shaft. The split-tube design (bottom) has six spacers with a 1-inch countershaft. You may run into other combinations, such as a solid 1-inch tube with four spacers. Set the countergear up to have the end spacers slightly below the countergear end, usually 0.010 to 0.020 inch per side. Too much clearance can cause the needles to skew. Spacers running too tightly can jam up the needles.

Assembly

AGE Supercase

We are installing the new Auto Gear Equipment supercase (left), which has thicker and stronger mounting ears. It takes a wider front-sealed bearing and has a sealing plug for the countershaft. This resolves the Muncies' common problem of leaking from the front.

1 Install the Front Thrust Washer

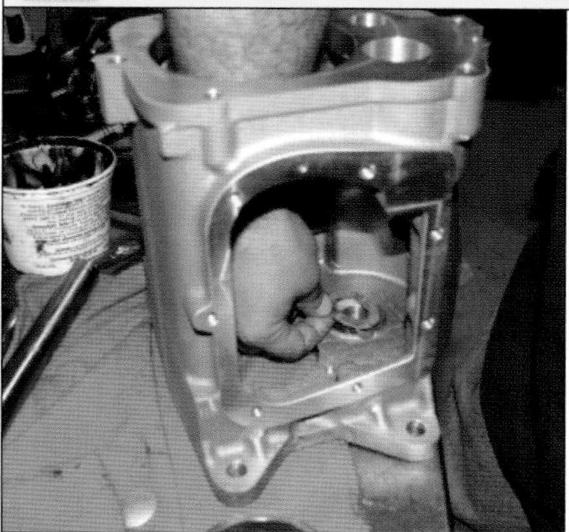

Start assembly with the case face down, and install the front thrust washer.

Professional Mechanic Tip

2 Place Countergear on Thrust Washer

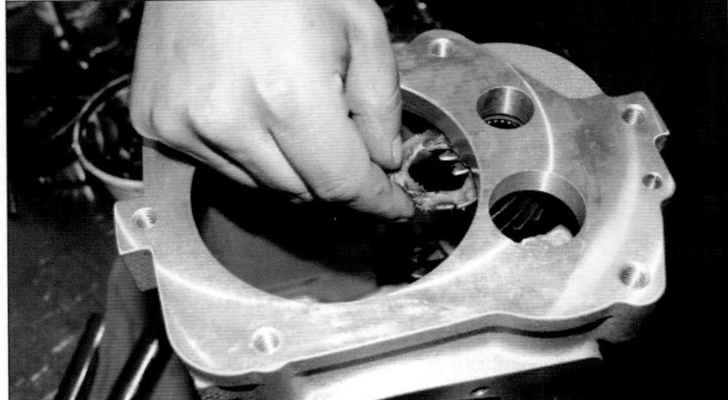

Drop the countergear in the case, resting it on the front thrust washer. Slip the rear washer between the gear and the case. This technique prevents pushing the thrust washers out of place if the countergear is sitting sideways. It also allows you to see that the washers are in place. Use enough assembly grease to hold washers in place.

Sealed Front Bearings

The newer-style sealed front bearing is on the left. You can see how much wider it is compared to the older style on the right.

3 Install Solid Slingers

Install solid slingers (new style) rather than tanged slingers (old style). Older-style slingers tend to have tangs that break off. This also acts as a 0.030-inch spacer. The new case design also corrects sloppy alignment of the input and countershafts.

Professional Mechanic Tip

4 Install Input Shaft

Most books direct rebuilders to install the countergear first. Instead, I suggest you leave the countergear dropped down and install the input shaft with the bearing. As a result, you won't drive the front bearing on with a hammer while the geartrain is in place and damage the fourth-gear synchro ring.

5 Install Countershaft

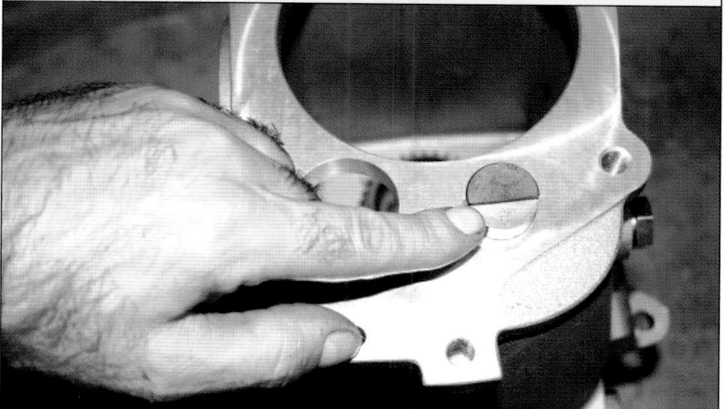

Install the countershaft with the flat side facing this position.

6 Use Old Main Case

Here is a trick to assembly a Muncie: Place it on an old case so that you can work at a comfortable level and still keep the input shaft pointing down.

7 Grind a Taper on Reverse Idler Gear

Try grinding more of a taper to the reverse idler gear, so it never hits the 1-2 slider.

8 Insert Needles in Input Cage

Needles must be held in with grease on the input cage. They are positioned in place on the outside of the cage.

9 Complete Main Case

The main case prep has been completed when the input, needles, synchronizer ring, and idler washer have been installed along with a freshly ground idler gear.

Important!

10 Position Synchro Hubs

Positioning synchro hubs the wrong way is a common mistake. To position them correctly, both hubs must have their extended bosses facing toward the front.

11 Install 1-2 Slider

The sliders, however, face in opposite directions. The 1-2 slider's taper faces the rear and the 3-4 sliders taper faces the front. For complete synchro ring assembly instructions, refer to page 26.

12 Press Second Gear and Parts onto Shaft

Place the second gear and its synchro ring onto shaft. Next, place the 1-2 assembly and the first-gear sleeve, and press it into place as a unit. Make sure that they all locate correctly on the spline, and that the strut keys are indexed correctly in the synchro ring.

13 Install First Gear Synchro Ring and Parts

Install the first-gear synchro ring, first gear, the mid-plate assembly, rear bearing snap ring, and upper reverse gear.

14 Position Speedometer Gear

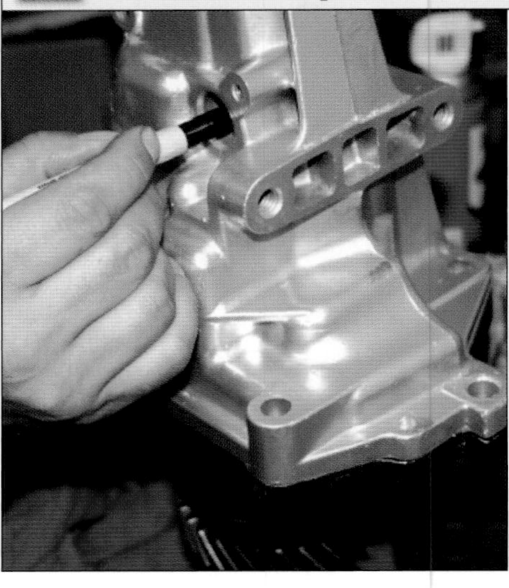

An easy way to determine correct speedometer gear position is to make sure it is close to or on center in the speedo hole of the tail. Put the tail in place and use a felt-tip marker to indicate the center point on the shaft.

15 Heat and Slide Gear into Position

The gear is heated up until it turns blue/brown. When it reaches the correct color, slide it into the correct position with a pair of pliers. Since the gears are soft, this technique avoids damage to the surface.

16 Install Third Gear and Parts

Install third gear, the third-gear synchro ring, synchro assembly, and snap ring on the front part of the mainshaft.

17 Install Reverse Detent Spring and Ball

Once you have installed a new bushing and seal in the tail section, install the reverse detent spring and ball, which are held in place with grease. Hold them down with a pry bar and slide the reverse shifter shaft in place. You can also heat up and bend a small putty knife to make a similar tool.

18 Install Shifter Shaft Seal

Once the shaft is in place, install the shifter shaft seal. Do this last, so you're not fighting the seal's resistance against the shifter shaft. This procedure actually reduces possible damage to the seal. Once the seal is over the shaft, seat it in place with a deep socket.

19 Install Reverse Shifter Fork

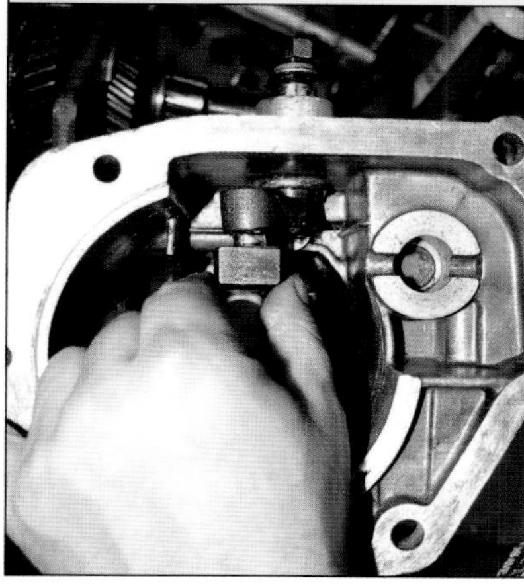

Place the reverseshift fork in position with grease. Fasten it with either a nut and washer or bolt, depending on the year transmission on the shift shaft. Rotate the shaft in a forward position. The nut and bolt keep the shaft from popping out.

20 Position 3-4 Slider

Position the 3-4 slider slightly forward to install the mainshaft assembly in the main case.

21 Guide Mainshaft Over Countershaft

Hold the 3-4 slider in place and guide the mainshaft over the countergear. This is a difficult procedure since we are dealing with parts, and you have to also make sure the fourth-gear ring indexes correctly with the 3-4 synchro assembly.

Important!

As you get over the countergear, pull the 3-4 slider back into position, making sure the mid plate dowel is correctly aligned, then sink it all in place.

22 Install Rear Reverse Idler and Parts

Install the rear-reverse idler, thrust washer, and idler shaft in the main case. Align the shaft so that the roll pin faces in this position. Notice the "skin" coats of sealant.

Professional Mechanic Tip

23 Install Tailhousing Main Case

Install the tail by catching the reverse fork on the reverse gear. Once caught, tap in the shifter shaft with your palm, mate the tail to the main case, and bolt it up.

24 Install Reverse Shifter Shaft Locking Pin

From the top, drive in the reverse shifter shaft locking pin.

25 Tighten Input Shaft to Main Case

Tighten the front nut with either Channel Locks or a special front nut wrench. You can use a little thread locker on the threads. Remember, these are left-handed threaded nuts. Always use a new nut in a rebuild because this functions as a front seal. You have to lock the transmission in two gears at once to keep the input from spinning.

26 Use Sealant on Retainer Bolts

If you are using factory lock plates or stand-alone bolts, always use sealant on the threads. It acts as a thread locker as well.

27 Install Front Retainer

The front retainer is installed with the lock plate tangs bent. The Auto Gear Supercase uses a soft plug on the front of the countershaft. It takes very little pressure to press it in place.

Important!

28 Rotate Transmission and Check Operation

Now is a good time to stick in an old driveshaft yoke and rotate the transmission to see that everything is working smooth, not binding, and shifting. I always splash a little gear lube on the gears when I do this.

Needle Bearings in Side Cover

The new Auto Gear side cover uses needle rollers in the side cover. Most older factory covers are extremely sloppy here. Elongated bores cause leaks and geometry problems, which lead to poor shift feel and quality. The rollers keep the shift shafts supported firmly.

29 Deburr Detent

Deburr all detent combs on new and used units with a Dremel cutoff wheel. Check for worn combs. Also note the position of the detent spring. If positioned in this manner, it can never fall into the transmission.

Torque Fasteners

30 Install Side Cover

Place both the transmission and side cover in second gear. This allows the 1-2 fork to clear the reverse idler boss in the main case. Once in place, align the dowel in the case and tighten the bolts to 18 ft-lbs.

BONUS CONTENT:
Scan to learn about Muncie 4-speed rebuilding upgrades.

31 Install Speedometer Fitting

The final step is to install the speed fitting. Older fittings had no seals. The new ones do. Don't bother fixing a rusted leaking fitting, when a new one costs under $10.

Here is the complete build with new hardware. Unless I'm restoring a transmission that requires certain logos on bolts, new grade-5 or grade-8 hardware is preferable. You don't have to spend time cleaning the hardware, and you don't risk bolts breaking.

FORD TOPLOADER 4-SPEED TRANSMISSION

The Toploader's top cover and side-mounted shifter shafts distinguish it from all other American 4-speed designs. Although there were some 3-speed transmissions manufactured, the Toploader 4-speed loaded the geartrain from the top. The T10, Muncie, Saginaw, and Chrysler A833 all used a side cover.

It is also interesting to note that this transmission used a 3-shift rail design. The shift rails kept the shift forks moving in the exact same plane as the synchronizers. All other transmissions were designed with the forks moving in an arc, and these side-cover designs allowed for more shift-fork play. The Toploader design maintains a better shift-fork geometry, reducing wear and contributing to a better shift feel.

Ford, just like GM, used a T10 4-speed. The Toploader was introduced in Ford cars in 1964. There are several years in which both the T10 and Toploader were actually used within the same platform. The passenger-car Toploader came in three different case lengths and several spline configurations. Output shafts in early 1964–1965 cars had weak 25-spline output shafts. Later, these were revised to 28-spline output shafts.

Engines with 200 to 390 ci got 1$\frac{1}{16}$-inch-diameter, 10-spline input shafts whereas the 427-, 428-, and 429-ci engines came with a huge 1 3/8-inch-diameter, 10-spline input shaft. In fact, this is the largest-diameter input shaft ever used in a passenger car manual transmission. The "big input" mainshafts also had 31-spline "big-output" transmissions.

There are many variations of main cases and extension housings sporting individual and multiple bolt patterns for shifter and engine mounting. By the mid 1970s, Tremec took over manufacturing this transmission for Ford. Overdrive versions appeared as early as 1977 in the Ford Granada and Mercury Monarch. Overdrive versions with shifters mounted on side turrets as well as top covers were made with alloy cases.

Both 10-spline input shafts can handle incredible horsepower loads from big-block engines. A 1$\frac{3}{8}$-inch-diameter shaft is shown on the left and a 1$\frac{1}{16}$-inch shaft is on the right.

Identification of Toploader models can be confusing. After all these years, few transmissions actually have remained untouched. Most units I find have been built from bits and pieces, making it harder to distinguish what was or was not original. The Toploader had more than 100 different models based on engine, vehicle, and year. Two basic ratios were offered. The wide-ratio features a 2.78 first, 1.93 second, 1.36 third, and direct fourth. The other was the close-ratio with a 2.32 first, 1.69 second, 1.29 third, and direct fourth. The close ratio was the only ratio offered with the large-style input and output shafts. Today, you can purchase aftermarket wide-ratio input shafts in the larger style.

Left to right: 25-, 28-, and 31-spline output shafts.

Tags fastened to the passenger side of the transmission tell what make and model the transmission was used in. Tags starting with the letters HEH- followed by two additional letters are typical of early 1964–1966 Models. The RUG designator was introduced in 1967 and continued into 1986. All RUG models from 1977-up are overdrive models. Top cover versions used in Bronco have the RTS designator.

Transmission Build-Up

I decided to build up a Ford Toploader using the latest upgrades available. In this build we are going to transform a tired, rusty transmission into a lightweight powerhouse.

Common Mainshaft Failure

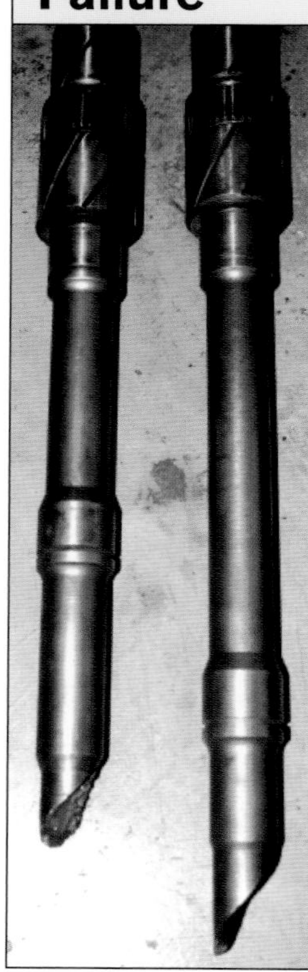

Here is a common 25-spline mainshaft (right) and one with a failure (left). Often, these early 25-spline designs did not survive the shock loads of power shifts nor starting-line clutch dumps. The 28- and 31-spline mainshafts were a big improvement.

Disassembly

1 Remove Top Cover

The bearing retainer and top cover are removed. The front bearing had exploded in this transmission, and all that was left of it was the inner race. This ruined the front bearing bore of the case.

2 Remove Detent Spring

With the top cover off, some units have the 1-2 detent spring exposed. Sometimes it is held down with a screw. Remove the spring and fish out the detent with a magnet.

3 Remove Set Screws

Remove both set screws for the 1-2 and 3-4 forks.

4 Remove 3-4 Detent Bolt

Remove the 3-4 detent bolt, spring, and detent. Again, fish them out with a magnet.

5 Remove Tailhousing

Remove the four tailhousing bolts and slide the tailhousing off. Be careful not to damage the plastic speedo drive gear.

6 Take Off Speedometer Gear

Remove the speedometer gear snap ring, and slide the gear off. Use a magnet and remove the anti-rotation check ball that is under the gear.

7 Remove Snap Ring

Remove the rear bearing mainshaft snap ring.

8 Pull 1-2 Shift Rail from Case

Once the set screw and detent have been removed from the 1-2 shift rail, slide the rail out of the back of the case.

9 Punch Countershaft Out of Case

Punch the countershaft out of the case from front to rear.

Professional Mechanic Tip

10 Remove Countergear Shaft from Case

Flip the transmission over so it is lying top down. This takes the load off the countergear and allows the shaft to be easily removed. Don't be concerned about needle bearings falling out of the case. New ones are in the rebuild kits. If you are reusing them, you may want to lay the whole assembly in a flat pan.

11 Pull Input Shaft Out of Case

Flip the transmission back over. The countergear will drop down, allowing the input shaft to be pulled out of the front. Tilting the whole transmission front face downward may help keep the maindrive needle bearings from falling out of the input shaft.

12 Tap Mainshaft Out of Case

Use a soft hammer to push the mainshaft out of the rear bearing. With the countergear dropped, you can almost get the rear bearing completely removed.

13 Push Main Bearing Out of Case

Use a bearing clamp to support the rear bearing. This allows you to push the mainshaft out of the rear bearing completely.

14 Pry Rear Bearing Out of Case

Pry the rear bearing out of the case using screwdrivers or pry bars.

15 Remove 1-2 Shift Fork

Once the rear bearing and front input have been taken out of the case, you have the necessary clearance to remove the 1-2 shift fork.

16 Remove 3-4 Shift Rail

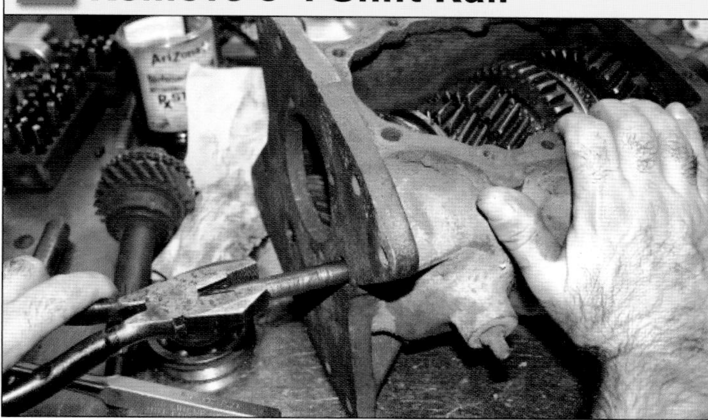

Remove the 3-4 shift rail by tapping it from the rear and pulling it out from the front. Once the rail has been removed, remove the 3-4 fork as well.

17 Retain Interlock Pin

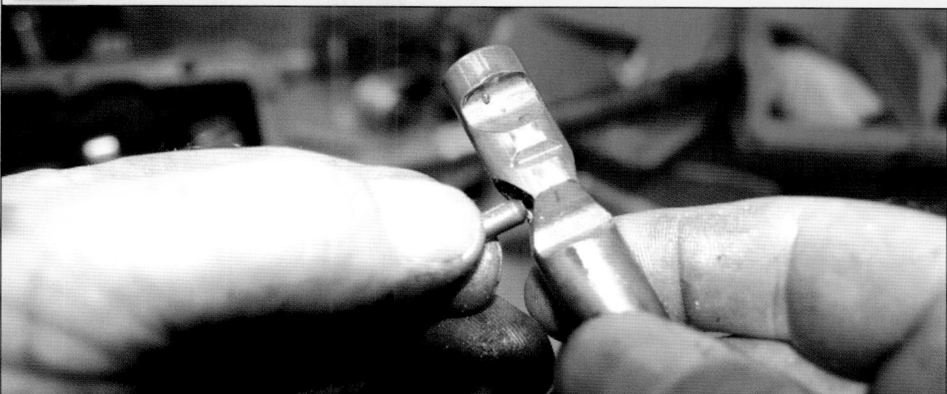

Professional Mechanic Tip

PRO TIP

The 3-4 rail has an interlock pin. Make sure you don't lose this pin. The interlocks that sit above and below this rail may fall out as well. If you don't want to remove them at this time, stuff the center rail support with a paper towel.

18 Remove Geartrain

With both forks and rails removed, it is now possible to remove the entire geartrain. Be careful not to catch your fingers in the case—these parts are very heavy.

19 Remove Countergear

Now that the geartrain is removed, the countergear can be removed as well.

20 Remove Detents

Spraying the detent/interlock bores with WD40 may allow you to remove the detents more easily. Oil deposits and sludge usually can make them difficult to remove.

21 Remove Rail Set Screw

Unless the reverse idler gear is damaged, rarely does this assembly need to be removed during a rebuild. To start, remove the rail set screw.

22 Pull Reverse Rail from Case

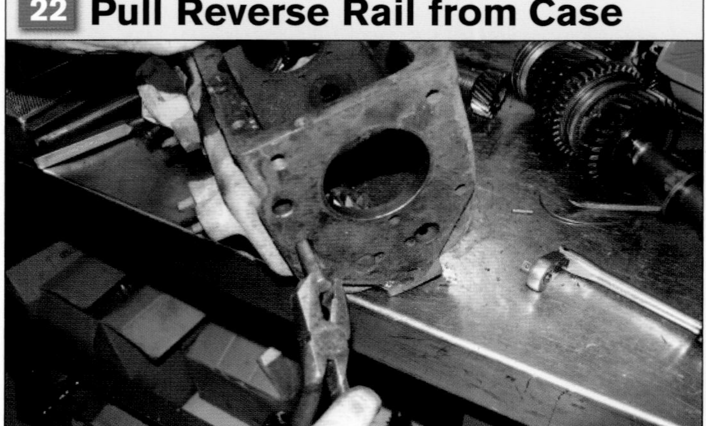

Remove the reverse rail by rotating it 90-degrees clockwise to dislodge it from its own detent. Pull the rail and fork out of the case. Remove the reverse detent and spring.

23 Remove Shifter Shaft

Since all the rails have been removed, it is now possible to remove all the shifter shafts. Be sure to mark which ones go in which places.

24 Remove Reverse Idler Shaft

Remove the reverse idler shaft by tapping it from the front and then by pulling it out from the back. When removing this last component from the case, notice the orientation of the sliding idler gear in relation to the main idler.

Documentation Required

25 Note Orientation of Parts

Putting parts back in the wrong place causes most building errors. Notice the difference between the 3-4 fork on the left and the 1-2 fork on the right.

Documentation Required

26 Remove First Gear from Main Shaft

Pull the first gear and first-gear thrust washer off the mainshaft. Notice the direction of the 1-2 slider.

Critical Inspection

27 Remove 3-4 Synchro and Parts

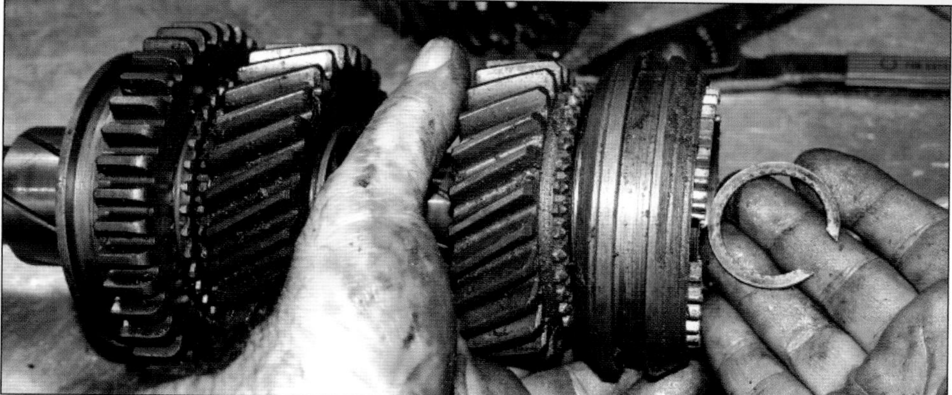

Remove the 3-4 synchro snap ring, 3-4 synchronizer, and third gear. Also inspect the tip of the mainshaft for galling and wear.

28 Remove Second Gear and Parts

Remove the second-gear snap ring, snap-ring spacer, and second gear.

29 Remove 1-2 Synchro and Parts

Remove the 1-2 synchro snap ring and 1-2 synchro assembly. Notice the orientation of the 1-2 synchro hub. The thin edge faces towards second gear.

Important!

30 Install Strut Synchro Keys

The most common mistake in Toploader rebuilds is mixing up the synchro strut keys or dogs. The longer key on the right is the 1-2 key; the one on the left is the 3-4 key. New 1-2 keys are notched to distinguish them from 3-4 keys. Putting the long key on the 3-4 synchro will cause the unit to lock up on final assembly.

Critical Inspection

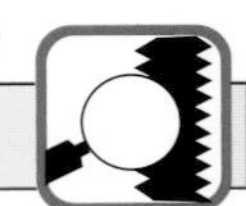

31 Inspect Components

Another overlooked wear point is the key slots. Over time, keys pound out of the slots. The pounded-out key allows the synchro ring to rotate farther than it should, and this causes a block-out shift condition. The unit requires a completely new assembly on both 3-4 and 1-2 because of this.

Both second and third gears have badly worn and broken engagement teeth. This is very common in the Toploader design. The new, modern gears have longer teeth with torque-locking angles.

This input shaft front bearing has badly damaged the gear teeth, and this gear is just too rusty.

Final Assembly

Assembling the Toploader is basically a reversal of the disassembly techniques. I have noticed that some units have different-shape detents with a flat edge rather than conical-shape interlock pins. Other units have the same-size conical-shape interlocks and detents and still others may have different lengths. It is best to lay everything out on a flat surface and pre-fit the rail system to make sure it works properly. I find it is better to test the rail system first without anything in the way so that it is quite easy to make corrections, rather than have to remove gears and start over.

Assembly

Professional Mechanic Tip

1 Deburr and Polish Shift Rails

PRO TIP

Deburr and polish the shift rails. Most interlocks and detents groove and burr the shafts, so deburr and polish each rail and make sure they glide smoothly in the case.

Use of Aftermarket Case

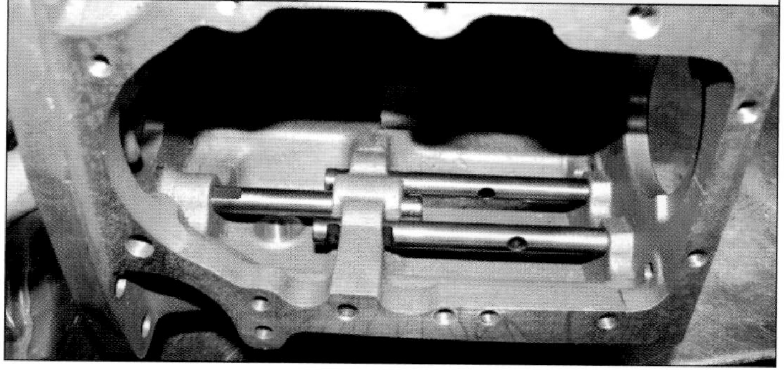

We are using a new David Kee case. Be sure to prefit all polished and deburred shift rails in the case.

Interlock System Components and Tools

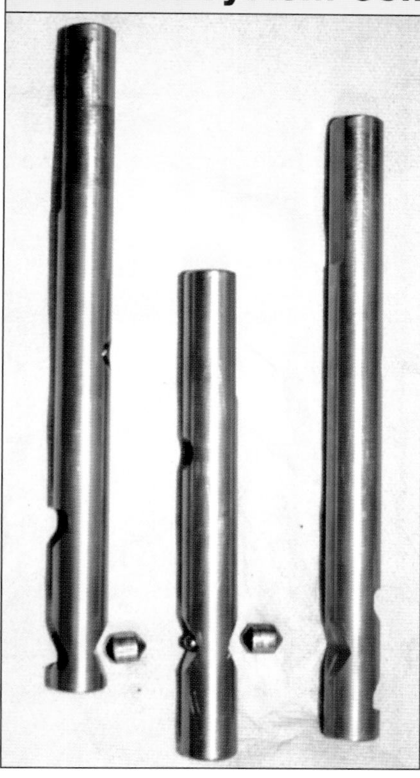

This is basically how the interlock system works: When any one rail is moved, the interlock pin is raised, preventing any other rail from moving.

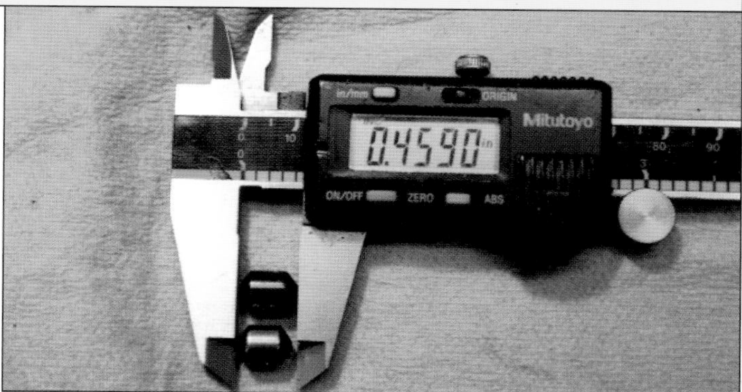

You can see that the detent pin is longer than the interlock pin. If you mix them up, the unit will not shift.

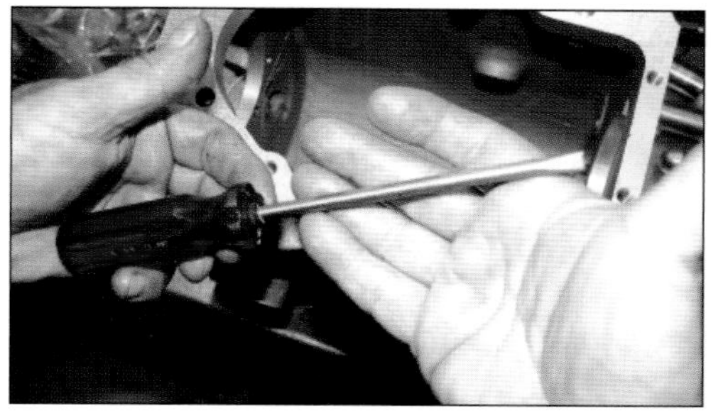

Use a long screwdriver with a flattened tip as a tool to install detents and interlocks.

2 Drill and Tap Case

Some cases have a 1-2 detent spring that is held in place by the cover. I drill and tap the case and make my own detent hold-down. I like this method better because I can fully test the transmission with the top cover off.

Toploader Rebuild Kit

Many companies sell a typical small-parts kit. Never throw out your old small parts. This kit had no front bearing snap ring, and the countergear needle spacers were the wrong size. The new thrust washers are nylon instead of bronze. Fortunately, these are actually what the newer units use, so they will be fine.

3 Install Reverse Idler

Insert the new needles and spacers in the reverse idler assembly. Place the rear thrust washer in the case first and keep it in place with grease. It is easy to place the forward thrust washer in last after the idler shaft is supporting the idler assembly and rear washer.

4 Install Shifter Shafts

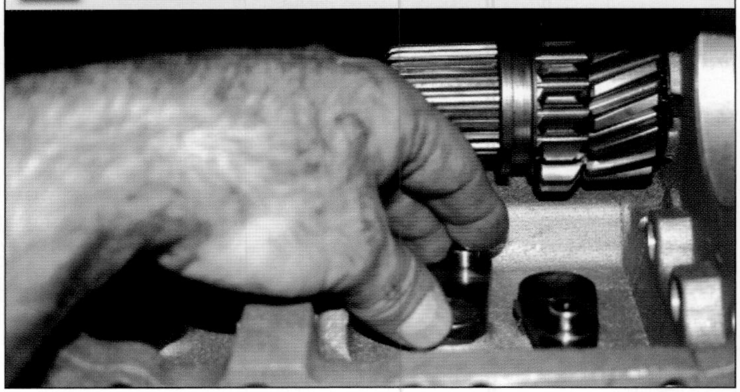

After installing the reverse idler assembly, you can install the three shifter shafts with their new O-rings. Notice that the longer reverse shifter shaft faces down.

5 Install Reverse Springs

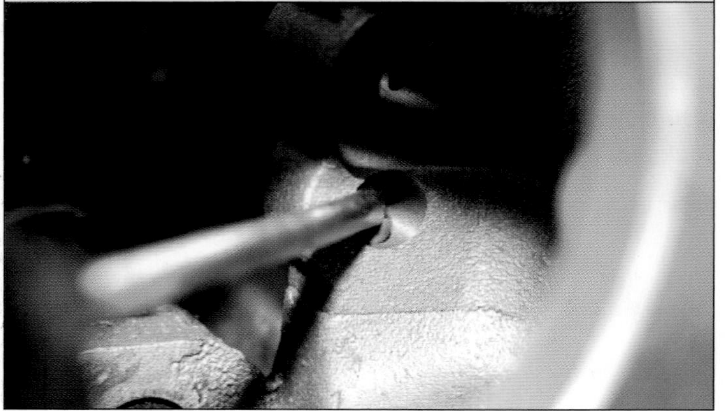

Install the reverse spring and move the detent into place with your "tool."

6 Install Reverse Fork and Rail

From the top, compress the detent down and install the reverse fork and rail into place. Once in place, reinstall the reverse fork set screw.

7 Install 3-4/Reverse Pin

Before installing any other gears, it is easier to install the 3-4/reverse interlock pin. Use your special tool to get it into the bore.

8 Place Countergear in Case

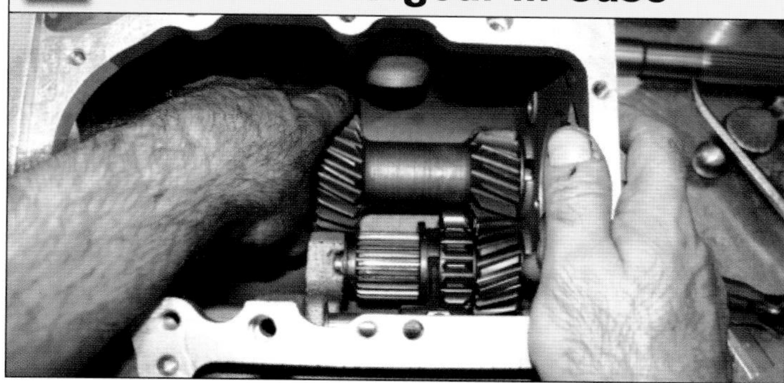

Install the needles and spacers in the countergear and install the thrust washers as well. Drop the countergear in the case, making sure the washers stay aligned properly with the countershaft bore while the gear is sitting as low as possible.

9 Position Strut Springs

Important!

Both strut springs' "hump" needs to be located on the same strut key in every synchro assembly. For complete synchro ring assembly instructions, refer to page 26.

10 Install 1-2 Synchro Assembly

Install the 1-2 synchro assembly and snap ring, second gear, second-gear snap-ring spacer, and second gear snap ring on the main shaft.

11 Install Third Gear

Now install the third gear, third-gear synchro ring, the 3-4 synchro assembly, and 3-4 synchro snap ring. Some transmissions have tighter fits than others when it comes to installing synchro assemblies.

12 Install First Gear Snap Ring and Parts

Flip the whole mainshaft assembly over and install the first-gear snap ring, first gear, and first-gear thrust washer.

13 Install Mainshaft into Case

The new case as well as old cases have a relief for the 1-2 slider to clear. My thumb is keeping first gear in place.

14 Install 3-4 Rail Interlock

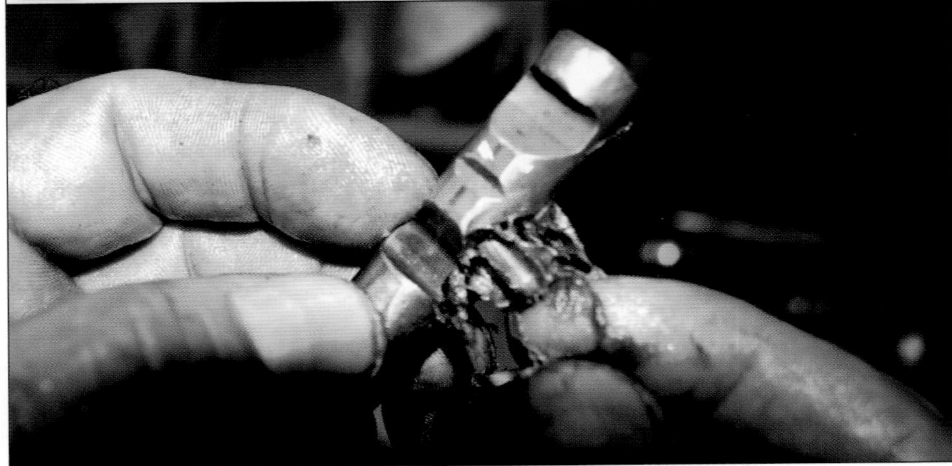

Hold the 3-4 rail interlock in place with grease.

15 Slide 3-4 Rail into Position

Important!

Locate the 3-4 fork on the shifter shaft and slide the 3-4 rail into place. Make sure to keep the rail positioned with the set-screw hole facing up.

16 Install Forks and Position 1-2 Shifter Shaft

Drop the interlock in that sits between the 3-4 rail and the 1-2 rail. Position the 1-2 fork on its shifter shaft, and slide the 1-2 rail in from the back. With both forks in place, lock them in place with the set screws. Factory screws had nylon locking inserts, which may be worn. You can use blue liquid threadlocker instead.

17 Reposition Case

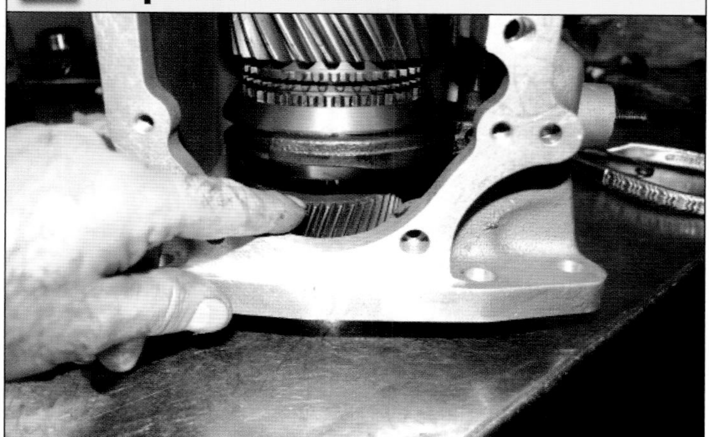

Flip the case on its front. Use something to keep the upper geartrain in place, such as an older pinion gear.

18 Press Bearing into Case

You can use a punch or pipe to press the rear bearing in place. Install both inner and outer snap rings.

19 Install Steel Gear

Performance Tip

Because the plastic gear strips out all the time, Auto Gear has reproduced the common seven-tooth gear in steel, which is similar to the black-nylon gear. It saves you the headache of pulling a transmission for a $25 part.

20 Install Check Ball on Main Case

Install the check ball on the mainshaft. Slide the speedometer gear in place and secure it with a snap ring.

21 Install Fourth-Gear Synchro Ring

Install the fourth-gear synchro ring from the front. Apply assembly lube on the ring and stick it in place.

Professional Mechanic Tip

PRO TIP

22 Install Input Shaft

The input shaft has some clutch teeth removed, so it can be installed from the front and clear the countergear. Position it so that the flat spot is facing the countergear.

Lay the transmission on its cover side. It makes installing the countershaft simple and fast. I'm using my left index finder to hold and feel that the countergear is in place.

23 Use Sealant for 3-4 Detent Bolt

My finger points to the 3-4 detent, and the screwdriver is on the 1-2 detent. Use sealant on the 3-4 detent bolt.

Torque Fasteners

24 Place Sealant on Housing Bolts

Some Toploaders require sealant on the extension housing bolts. Torque these bolts to 35 ft-lbs.

Performance Tip, Torque Fasteners

25 Install Front Retaining Bolts

The factory front retainer bolts have a serrated locking thread. These ruin the case threads, so regular grade-8 bolts were used with blue liquid threadlocker. Torque these bolts to 18 ft-lbs. Don't forget to install the 11/16-inch case plug.

26 Install Top Cover

The top cover has bolts of two different lengths. The two longer bolts are placed in their correct positions.

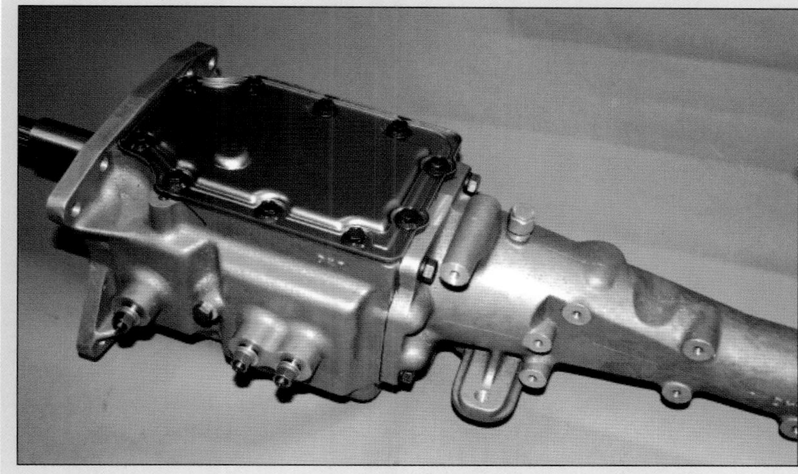

Here is the completed unit. Notice the special filtered vent I installed in the tail. The factory vent is that little bulged pinhole in the top cover.

Other Common Manual Transmissions

Although there are some transmissions that may or may not be suited for high-performance use, they need to be mentioned. There are also newer transmissions that are replacing the older muscle car ones that deserve discussion here as well.

Saginaw 4-Speed

This is a GM light-duty car transmission used from 1966 to 1985. It has a cast-iron case with all shift levers on the side cover. Often mistaken for a Muncie, it is sometimes labeled as one on Internet sites, such as eBay.

A Saginaw gear set is shown on the top; a Muncie, on the bottom. Notice how the 1-2 slider also is used as a reverse gear.

Richmond Gear 4+1 5-Speed

Originally designed and sold by Doug Nash, the fifth gear was not an overdrive, but a direct fifth. It allowed you to have a fairly high rear-end ratio of 3.08 and still have a close-ratio transmission capable of accelerating like a Muncie M21 with 4.11 gears. Richmond Gear has improved on the design, making a 6-speed called a ROD as well as a newer 5-speed with an overdriven fifth gear.

The cast-iron Saginaw has a seven-bolt side cover just like a Muncie, but it lacks a center support or mid plate.

A Muncie mainshaft is pictured above the weaker Saginaw 4-speed mainshaft.

The new Richmond Overdrive was released in 2007. Reverse is moved to the rear, and the gears are much wider than on the original 4+1 transmission.

A Richmond Gear 4+1 5-speed is installed in a 1967 Corvette. Note how the 3½ inch center-to-center makes the transmission overhang the bellhousing.

ZF S6-40

ZF Friedrichshafen AG is a leading worldwide supplier of manual transmissions. Founded in 1915, this company primarily produced transmissions for both the European industrial and automotive markets. By 1988 it developed a 6-speed transmission that GM used in the C4 Corvette platform starting in 1989. It replaced the weak Doug Nash 4+3 transmission used in the Corvette from 1984 to 1988. Many people use these in other applications but tend to forget that service parts are extremely expensive.

Tremec

Tremec had purchased Borg-Warner's manual-transmission division. This gave Tremec the right to produce the T5 and T56 6-speed. Tremec was already making the Ford Toploader and various overdrive and 2-wheel-drive versions of it for Mexican and South American truck markets.

A transmission called the 3550 started out as a replacement for the 170FS (Forward Shift) Toploader. It was a heavy-duty 5-speed version for that truck market. The engineers at Tremec thought that with a tailhousing change they could make it fit as a replacement for the weak T5 in Mustangs. The first 3350 used three different shifter locations and similar ratios to the Mustang production T5. However, it really wasn't any stronger, because the truck design used individual countergear speed gears held on the countershaft with a keyway. Liberty's High Performance Products started cutting extra keyways to beef up these units. It took several attempts to get it right. Tremec came out with a TKO version, then a TKO 500 and TKO 600. These were offered for both GM and Ford cars with mechanical and electronic speedometer pick ups and a redesigned shifter that can be flipped 180 degrees to fit both makes.

A cutaway of the S6-40 Corvette 6-speed shows its massive gears.

Doug Nash 4+3

The Doug Nash Engineering 4+3 manual 4-speed with automatic overdrive was used in 1984 to 1988 Corvettes only. It was a Super T10 4-speed bolted to a 2-speed automatic overdrive. These transmissions required a computer to kick the overdrive unit on and off. Two options were available: the MK2

Here is a cutaway of the TKO600. Unlike the T5 it has multiple shift rails.

The covers are places for additional shifters. The rear shifter can be flipped around for more versatility.

with a .68 overdrive and the MH5 with a .59 overdrive. These units had no provision for mounting a shifter or a conventional crossmember mount because the Corvette used a floor-mounted shifter and a beam that rigidly mounted the transmission to the rear axle. Because the unit requires an oil cooler and a computer control, most people considering these for a non-Corvette applications should use an alternative. It is hard to find service parts as well as qualified people to work on them.

Auto Gear M33 "Syracuse 5-Speed"

Auto Gear was founded in 1945 by Irving H. Sollish and is currently under the leadership of his grandson, George Sollish. George pioneered the heavy-duty replacement cases, optional gear ratios, and the manufacture of a completely new replacement Muncie 4-speed, also known as the Model 18.

The M33 5-speed overcomes some unique design challenges. Perhaps the biggest one is to replace

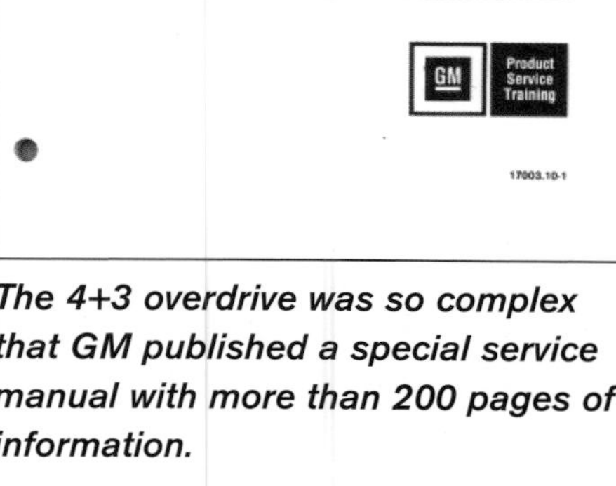

The 4+3 overdrive was so complex that GM published a special service manual with more than 200 pages of information.

a Muncie 4-speed and keep it as close to the same footprint. Most replacement 5-speeds suffer from lackluster shifting due to increased mass combined with increased center-to-center distances. The M33 keeps the original GM Muncie centers and incorporates synchronizers on the countergear to decrease shift effort.

This is the Viper version of the T56 6-speed. A similar version is also in the Corvette and Aston Martin.

CHAPTER 8

High-Performance Transmissions

Automatic transmissions obviously shift for you, and as a result, there are no missed shifts with an automatic. If you use an automatic transmission coupled to a torque converter, you will in most cases see more horsepower loss at the rear wheels compared to a manual transmission.

There are, however, many factors that determine winning a race other than rear-wheel horsepower loss. Missing a shift in a drag race will cost you the race no matter how efficient your gearbox is. Unless you can step up to a dependable and consistent manual transmission for drag racing, sometimes it is cheaper and more cost-effective to go with an automatic.

Road racing is another story. There are many gear ratios needed to negotiate various race tracks. Daytona may require a different set of ratios compared to Sebring. In a road-race environment, automatic design does not allow for quick ratio changes, quick tear-down, or the availability of efficient 4-, 5-, 6-, or even 7-speeds.

Endurance events, such as NASCAR-style racing, require designs to be as light and efficient as possible. With the newer style of metal alloys available today combined with the state-of-the-art CNC machining and 3D modeling, gear design has evolved to a level that allows for stronger horsepower capacity within a smaller configuration.

In a typical synchronized 4-speed, such as a Muncie, T10, Chrysler, or Ford Toploader, the transmission has 36 engagement or clutch teeth on the gear. The matching slider that engages the gear has the same number of teeth. When spinning above 6,000 rpm, the surface speed of the gear and slider can be very different in certain ratios.

I always associate this with trying to place a stick through a picket fence while driving by that fence at 60 mph. If I'm standing still, I can stick it between the pickets, but if

The standard A833 slider ring featured 36 teeth, but Chrysler was the only one of the Big Three to offer an 18-tooth slick-shift slider ring. Every other tooth has been machined away to create the 18-tooth gear.

I'm driving by at 60 mph, the stick may bounce off the fence. However, if I remove every 10 pickets from the fence I can get the stick through the fence at 60 mph just as easily as if I were standing still.

So, getting back to those 36 engagement teeth, if I remove every other tooth on the gear and slider, I've effectively cut my surface speed in half. At 6,000 rpm I now have the surface speed of a 3,000-rpm shift. The downside is that the engagement teeth must carry double the load they were originally designed for. This technique is called "slick shifting." From the 1960s to the early 1980s, it was possible to find new sliders specifically made for slick shifting. You purchased the sliders and modified your own gears. In fact, you could purchase from Chrysler complete, new gearsets and sliders for the A833.

In the mid 1960s a tool-and-die-maker for Cadillac was trying to improve on the slick-shifting concept. His design revolutionized the way transmissions shifted, and his name became synonymous with drag-race transmissions. Joe Liberty slick shifted his friend's transmissions for drag racing. Reducing the number of clutch teeth from 36 to 18 may have increased shift speed, but it promoted more wear. So he invented the "pro-shift" ring. The ring decreased the number of clutch teeth to 12 but increased the width, giving them back their holding power.

By 1972, business was so good that Joe left Cadillac Motors and started Liberty's High Performance Products. Liberty patented the concept of the pro-shift ring as a modification to a factory gear by grinding off the old engagement teeth and welding a new pro-shift ring. Next modified a Chrysler A833 with clutchless gears and won best-engineered product at the 1974 SEMA Show. These transmissions were made with completely new gears, which was also a first because few people back then had the resources to do such a thing. However, the transmission was not allowed in its intended racing class because the rulemakers thought it would give Chrysler an unfair advantage.

Stock Muncie input on the left, and one modified with Liberty's Pro Shift Ring on the right.

The modified A833 was only allowed in a class that it really wasn't designed for. This led to gear breakage. One day Joe was sitting at his desk rolling around some gears and watched three gears roll against one another. He came up with a new idea, paving the way for the first dual-cluster gear transmission. By putting the mainshaft between two countergears, mainshaft deflection is avoided and the load of the transmission is split between the two gears. This design increased the strength by 2.8 times.

The significance of Joe Liberty's concepts and designs sometimes went unnoticed. He was also the first to "combo" gears. Grinding off the countergear's headgear is the first step of the process. To create a different ratio he cut the head gear off from another countergear and combined the two by welding them together. I sold many gears made like this and can vouch that the welds never broke. When I asked Joe how he found someone to weld gears, he replied, "In Detroit there was an abundance of talent. You could find anyone to make anything. That's just how things were done."

Today, because of advanced alloys combined with CNC machinery, a multitude of performance transmissions are made with some unique designs. Because most of these transmissions are not mass-produced every gear starts as a piece of bar stock.

Racing transmissions can be shifted in a standard H-style pattern or a "sequential" pattern. A sequential pattern means you pull the stick in one direction for upshifts and in another direction for downshifts. There is no side-to-side movement; thus you don't have to worry about missing shifts because there are no gates. The concept basically is the same as a motorcycle transmission. A shift barrel rotates, and the rotation is translated into a linear movement of the shift fork.

Besides making transmissions with bigger components and stronger alloys, you can also use some of the techniques the big boys use on your everyday 4-speed. Deburrr all gears to get rid of high spots that can cause the slightest gear misalignment. Rarely do you find new gears that are not dinged. In the past, people have shot peened gears to add strength. Newer processes, such as Mikronite and Rem, chemically polish and peen gears. There are dry-film lubricant coatings available and the cryogenic treatment of gears, which can increase gear strength like a normal heat treatment would.

Very small companies have completely reproduced the Muncie, Toploader, and A833 4-speed. The costs to accomplish this would have been prohibitive 10 years ago. The quality and accuracy of the machine work far exceeds what was done 40 years ago. I expect this trend to continue as global markets open up and as unique and important designs materialize faster.

A JT5 Enduro gear has this removable dog ring faceplate. Notice how large the window is between the lugs. The larger window allows for higher RPM shifts.

A complete pro-shifted Muncie 4-speed utilizing new gears.

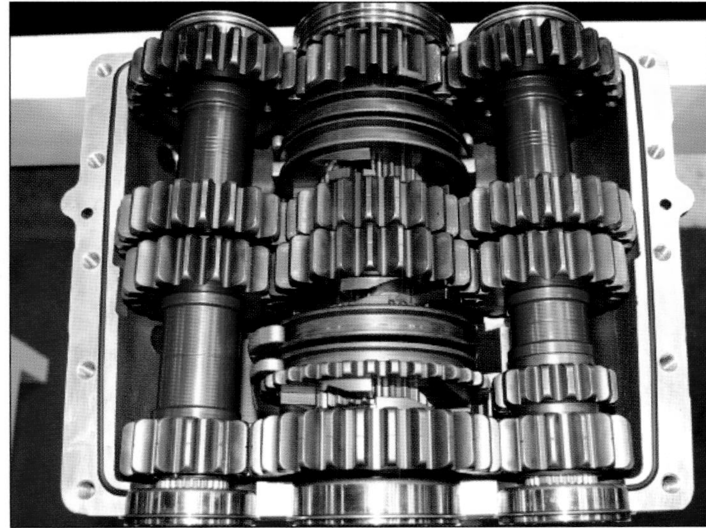

The latest version of a dual-countergear transmission increases load capacity by putting more gear teeth in contact with one another and splitting the load in half.

Because you are using two countergears, they must be timed. I'm pointing to the timing mark. The opposite gear has to be on the exact same tooth, or the transmission will lock up.

Bar stock cut for an input shaft made out of 9310VAR alloy.

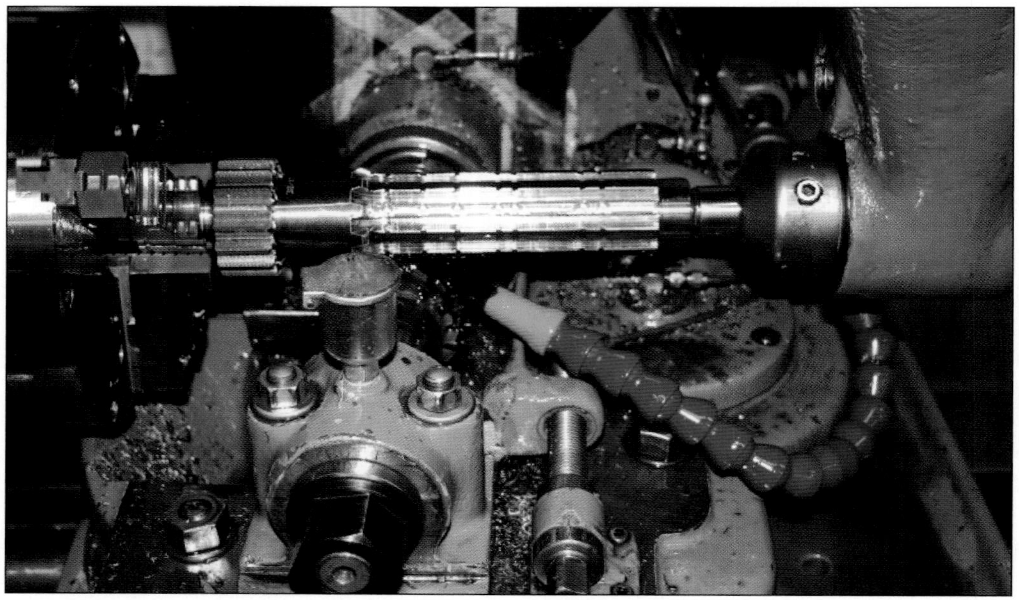

A G-Force racing countergear is being machined for a T5.

A Muncie 4-speed countergear that had broken first gear is recycled. The broken teeth are ground away to make a 3-speed dirt track transmission.

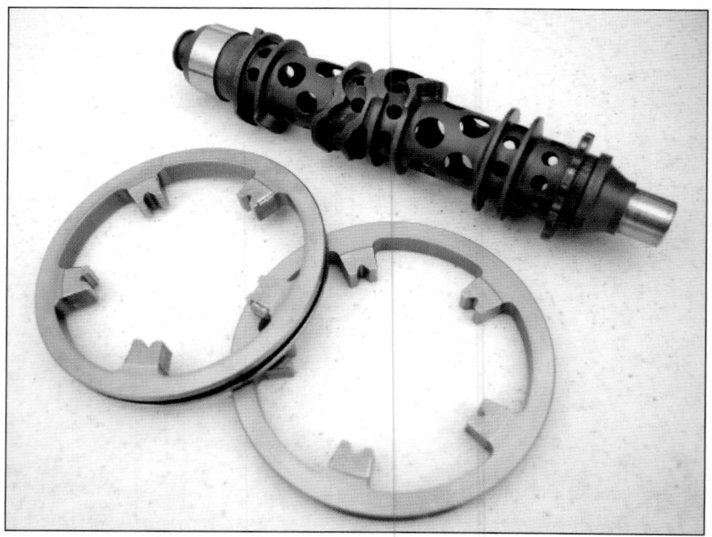

This shows the intricate machining of a Formula 1 titanium shift barrel and dog rings.

A transmission by Quaife uses a sequential barrel with dog-ring gears.

The Lenco transmission shifts by applying bands to lock the planetary gears in place. It's like manually shifting the bands of an automatic transmission.

The engagement teeth of a clutchless drag race transmission. Note how the dog teeth are ramped to pull themselves into gear.

In this Jerico air-shifted racing 5-speed, air is shuttled from one solenoid to another.

A JT5 Enduro 5-speed gear set is retrofitted into a stock T5 case.

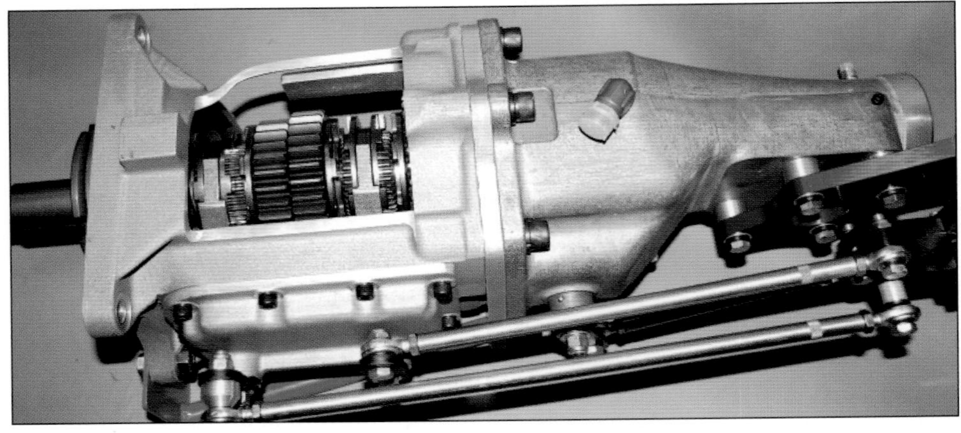

This Roltek T10 4-Speed is used for road racing with a Long Shifter.

This is a G-Force GF-2000 5-speed transmission. Notice the dual forks and slider for the clutchless operation. As one slider engages, the other is pulled from the opposite side.

This Hightower Racing transmission can actuate shift rods that are completely vertical, which makes this shifter unique and keeps the rods closer to the transmission's extension housing.

The G-Force GT-50 clutchless front-wheel-drive drag race transmission uses "Remmed" gears and a special Teflon dry-film coating on the case to promote oil flow.

The Muncie first gear on the right has been shot peened, deburred, and Mikronited.

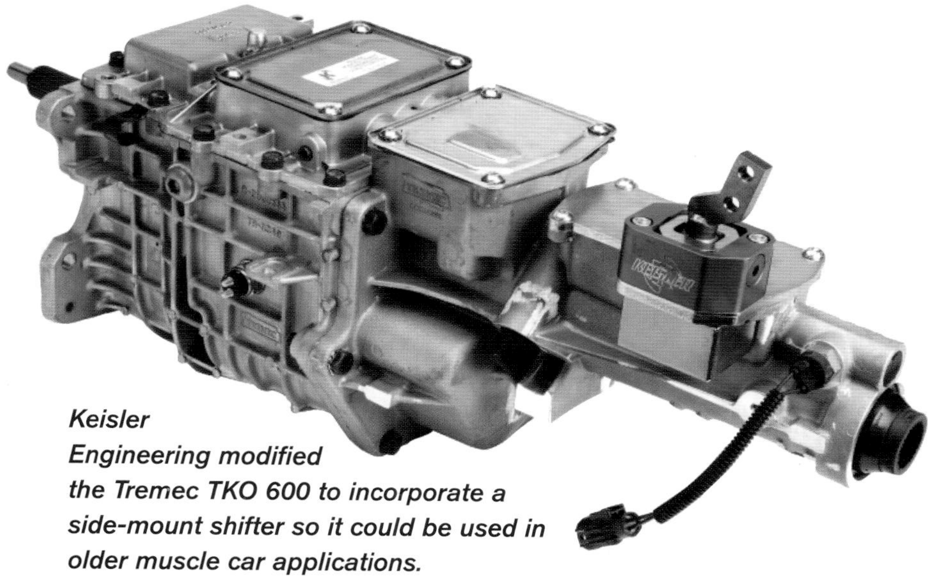

Keisler Engineering modified the Tremec TKO 600 to incorporate a side-mount shifter so it could be used in older muscle car applications.

The 5speeds.com Muncie SPEC25 uses the same coating as the G-Force GT-50. It's a fully synchronized transmission for race classes that require a synchronized transmission. The gears are also processed in the same fashion.

Clutch Basics

Although the focus of this book is manual transmissions, a transmission can be rendered useless without proper clutch performance. The premature failure of most synchronizers usually stems from some sort of clutch-related problem.

On any given week, I get a few calls about some sort of shifting issue. I ask the question, "Do you know how the clutch works?" The replies could fill a few chapters and appear humorous to some people, but the most common reply is "No."

You can think of the clutch as a simple on-and-off switch. Without it, the engine is connected to the transmission at all times. Power flow from the engine to the transmission would never be interrupted, and therefore, transmission gears and components would be loaded at all times. In order for a manual-transmission synchronizer to work properly, power flow has to be interrupted before and during the shift so that the synchronizer can work freely. This break in the power flow occurs when you press down on your clutch pedal. You turn the switch off.

Now the synchronizer can match gear speeds to the transmission output shaft with little effort. When this is accomplished, the shift is made, and power is reapplied by turning the switch on (lifting up on the clutch pedal).

Poor clutch release is the major cause of manual-transmission problems. Your on-and-off switch has become shorted. Frequent causes of poor release are simply not enough pedal travel or effective throw to cause a proper release.

Clutch Components

Your clutch system is made of six basic parts pilot bearing, bell housing, flywheel, release bearing, pressure plate, and clutch disc.

The pilot bearing, or pilot bushing, is installed in your engine's crankshaft. Its job is to keep the transmission input shaft concentric with the crankshaft centerline while allowing it to spin inside of it.

The bell housing locates the transmission to the engine. It also aids in keeping the transmission aligned with the engine. If you were to assemble a transmission to an engine with just a pilot bushing and bell housing, you would be able to spin the transmission freely while it maintains its concentricity with the crankshaft. The bell housing is located to the block with alignment dowels. "Dialing-in" a bell housing is the term for centering a bell housing with the crankshaft.

Offset dowels are often used to move the housing into spec. Most performance applications require run-out to be less than 0.008 inch while maintaining a parallel surface of 0.005 inch. If the housing is out of alignment, the transmission input shaft side loads and binds on the crankshaft pilot bearing, causing pilot bushing and front transmission bearing failure as well as clutch chatter and release issues.

The flywheel stores rotational energy. Heavy wheels may cause an engine to accelerate more slowly but allow smoother shifts because rpm does not fluctuate much. A lighter wheel may allow the engine to rev faster but may cause jerky off-the-line clutch chatter because of RPM flutter.

McLeod Industries produces an extremely light multi-disc clutch and flywheel.

Although most people don't associate release bearings, or throw out bearings, with the flywheel, they should. The flywheel is what the clutch pressure plate fastens to. If the height of the flywheel changes, the whole clutch assembly moves either closer or farther away from the release bearing. This is what typically happens when purchasing an aftermarket flywheel or having an older wheel resurfaced. Release bearings have pretty much been hydraulically activated since the mid 1980s. Resurfacing a flywheel with a hydraulic release bearing that has no adjustment causes most release issues. Mechanical linkages often compensate for these issues.

Clutch Types

At times it can be confusing as to what clutch you may need. Terms like "dual disc," "dual friction," "sprung hub," and "unsprung hub" don't make matters any easier.

I honestly don't understand most of the marketing hype surrounding clutches because a single-disc, organic-lined, diaphragm clutch has been used in many high-horsepower applications with a great life factor for many years. So why all the new technology?

The pressure plate, which is basically a clamp, ideally should have enough holding force for the intended application, yet be as easy to apply as possible. A certain amount of slippage should be required to avoid a jerky or harsh engagement. Harsh engagement can also lead to drivetrain breakage. The bigger the diameter the more the holding power, but the larger the diameter the more rotating mass. The new technology makes lighter, smaller clutches with great holding

Here is a McLeod hydraulic assembly mounted to a custom T5. Note that the line fittings swivel to allow you to fish the lines through the bell housing. Switching pistons, which come in several lengths, changes the adjustment.

Here is a cutaway of a Tilton hydraulic release bearing that mounts inside of the bell housing. Spacing it out or machining the housing provides adjustment.

power with the least amount of pedal effort.

Think of applying pressure to your chest with your finger as opposed to your hand. The finger applies the same pressure but with more pounds per square inch. It is easier to rotate your little finger compared to the whole palm with the same pressure behind it, so you would need more effortto keep your finger rotating than your whole palm. This is the principle behind the design of a dual-friction disc.

Generally, a diaphragm clutch weighs less than a Long-style or Borg & Beck-style. Long and Borg & Beck clutches are also known as "3-finger" clutches because the diaphragm is both the lever and the spring. Borg & Beck and Long-style clutches use three levers that push against a spring-loaded plate with coil springs. The Borg & Beck is not adjustable, while the Long-style is. Pedal pressure is easier with a diaphragm because of the lever ratio of 10:1. A Borg & Beck has a typical ratio of 6:1 and the Long-style 4.8:1. Height is a consideration because, obviously, the taller the clutch the longer the transmission's input shaft must be.

Clutch discs come in a wide variety of sizes, hubs, and linings. Most street applications have clutch discs that absorb initial shock in two ways. The first is the drive hub, which is driven by springs. The second is the surface of the lining, which is bonded to a wavy spring-steel surface commonly called a marcel.

The full cutaway shows the bearing on the left against a triple-disc 7-inch-diameter racing clutch.

Most new clutch designs are based on a typical diaphragm clutch like this one.

A Long-style clutch can be adjusted for more or less pressure.

The clutch drive plate will either be bolted or riveted to the lined surface. It is raised via stand offs to clear the sprung hub. The springs fit in the slots, which drive the plate. I'm removing the plate to expose the hub and springs.

People often have a hard time telling if a pilot bushing, throw-out bearing, or clutch is bad. In most applications (other than a Long-style), you cannot adjust for a slipping clutch. No external adjustment is going to help. The best method for adjusting correct release is to measure clutch release with a feeler gauge.

A typical, good release is 0.040 inch. Some bell housings have a lower inspection cover. You can usually place a feeler gauge between the flywheel and disc to get a measurement. This method is very accurate. Some people adjust a clutch by setting the amount of free play the pedal has before allowing the release bearing to make contact with the clutch. Using this method to adjust the clutch is actually the number-one cause of poor-release issues.

A quick down-and-dirty way to check for clutch release is to simply get the car good and warm so all components are heated and expanded. Press down on the clutch pedal and count to 10. Within 10 seconds the transmission should slow on its own. Most transmissions (the ones discussed in this book, anyway) have an unsynchronized reverse. If you try to put the transmission into reverse after the 10-second wait and the gears grind or clash, the transmission is still turning and has not been decoupled from the engine.

Here you can see the sprung hub. It mounts to the transmission input shaft and drives the transmission via the springs.

Here is the sprung hub on a transmission input shaft. This simple visual can give you a better idea of how power flow is put through a clutch system.

Here are some Ferrari racing clutches. The one on the right is a solid clutch with no marcel and no springs. The hub is riveted solid to the lining.

The organic side of a dual-friction disc with poly-encapsulated springs.

The Kevlar side of a dual-friction disc offers aggressive performance that's tame enough for street use.

The ClutchNet design locks the sprung hub to a solid drive plate. It uses more rivets and provides improved concentricity and strength. The springs act like little pistons absorbing shock loads.

The McLeod modular bellhousing allows for indicating the housing within itself because the mounting surface of the bellhousing is a separate component.

A Chevy bronze pilot bushing is on the left, and a factory roller-style pilot bearing is on the right. The needle-style bearing is less forgiving when a misalignment exists and can make a mess out of a crankshaft or input shaft if it fails.

Here is how a pilot bushing supports your input shaft. The correct support of this bushing and fit of a driveshaft yoke in the tail bushing are what keep things aligned.

CHAPTER 10

GUIDE TO SHIFTERS

Today most manual-transmission cars are equipped with a floor shifter. In general, prior to World War II, most vehicles had a shifter mounted in the top cover of the transmission. The shifter directly moved the shift forks. Automotive engineers in Detroit wanted to get away from floor-mounted shifters and create shifters built into the steering column. In order to create a column-mounted shifter, the actual transmission shift mechanism now had to have a series of external shifter shafts, linkage arms, shift rods, and levers for this design to be feasible. These new components required a redesign of the actual transmission to incorporate the addition of all these extra components.

This is the first sequential-style shifter design made for a side-rail-shifted transmission. The driver pulls one lever for upshifts and another for downshifts.

The column-shifter design was a far cry from the positive feel of the direct-top cover shifter. To provide that positive shift feel, modifying column shift back to a floor shift became the thing to do when drag racing started to flourish in the late 1950s. Drag racing puts a tremendous strain on linkage components, and a common modification was usually a custom floor shifter. Companies, such as Fenton, Sparkomatic, P&G, Hurst, and Mr. Gasket, were leaders in this field. The typical "H"-pattern shifter seems to have stood the test of time. The H-pattern design, for the most part, uses a horizontal gate. Thus, the shifter moves left or right to grab each gate.

Bill Bieber is the person credited with the design of the Vertigate Shifter. The gates were set up in a vertical alignment. This eliminated the need to move the shifter left or right. You just pulled the stick front to back to change gears. He also created a wild shifter, called "The Changer," which had two sticks. One was for upshifts and one for downshifts. You just pulled the sticks toward you to change gears. It used a huge rotating cam on the side cover.

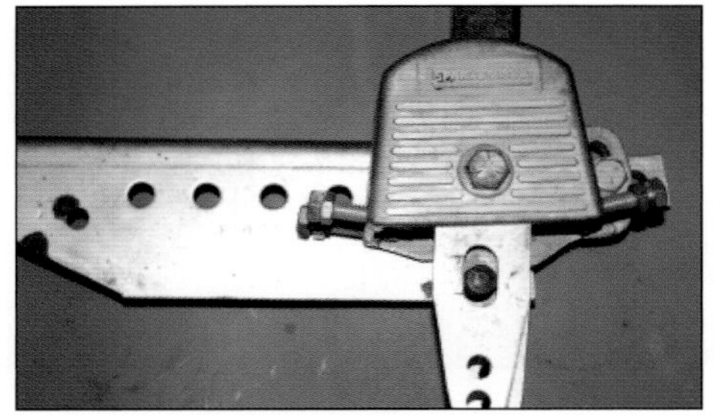

Thin stampings and cast-aluminum bodies made these early hot-rod-style shifters very weak.

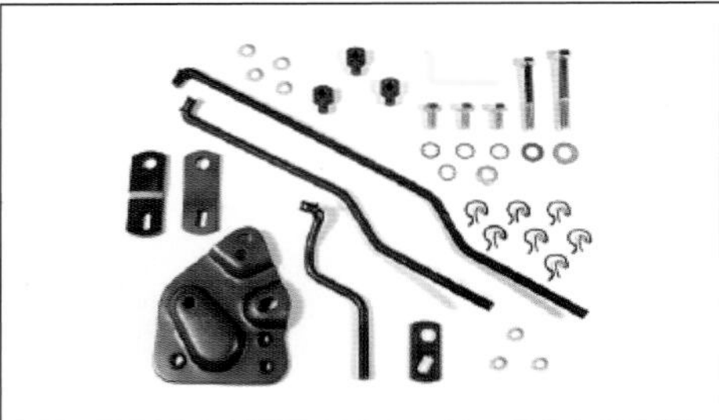

Hurst Shifters have a vast number of installation kits for just about every side-mounted 3- and 4-speed shifter.

Most of these designs suffered in the durability department, as well. The very popular Fenton and Sparkomatic incorporated die-cast aluminum bodies in some models, which quickly cracked under heavy use. The radically designed Changer required a huge portion of your floor pan to be cut out. Hurst and Mr. Gasket were the only two companies to survive the "shifter wars."

Various patents were issued protecting most of these unique shifter designs, and therefore only a handful of aftermarket companies specialized in this field. Today, things are much different. The T5 transmission has a multitude of companies making replacement shifters, and almost every high-end manufacturer has its own shifter.

The Hurst Competition Plus shifter improved on all previous designs, and it's still one of the best aftermarket shifters.

The Need for Shifters

All conventional factory linkage-style shifters lack the use of a stopping mechanism. For normal applications a "stop" may not be needed. When the "stop" isn't present, the force of your shift is stopped internally by the detents of the transmission. This leads to premature failure of shift detents, shift forks, or shift lugs. The stopping device is usually a bolt that is adjusted to absorb the force of the shift, thus extending the life of the internal components.

Improvement of shift "feel" is another important upgrade you should expect from a high-performance shifter. Usually they are designed to decrease travel lengthwise (short throw) and sometimes narrow the H-pattern. Others may incorporate a better left and right bias of the shifter.

The factory GM Muncie 4-speed shifter had no spring mechanism in the shifter other than to lift the reverse lock-out rod. Since it could flop left or right, it was clumsy to speed shift. You never knew the actual location of the shift gates.

The Hurst Competition Plus design has stood the test of time. It has a perfectly designed bias that keeps the handle in the 3-4 gate, so it aids you when going from second into third during speed shifting. It has an additional spring force to overcome when engaging reverse, eliminating reverse lockout levers. GM actually started to install these shifters in the 4-4-2 and GTO.

Here is a Long HN-1000 H-Pattern shifter designed for a Cobra kit car and bolted to a Richmond 5-speed.

The Long HN-1000 uses rails that run parallel with one another and in a straight line, as opposed to the Hurst shifter that has the gates move in an arc within the shifter body.

When it comes to road racing, Mid Valley Engineering's Shur Shifter is hard to beat. The whole mechanism is in a sealed housing. Basically, internal rails shift many transmissions, and the Shur Shifter can turn any external-linkage-designed transmission into a rail-shifted type with built-in stops and interlocks.

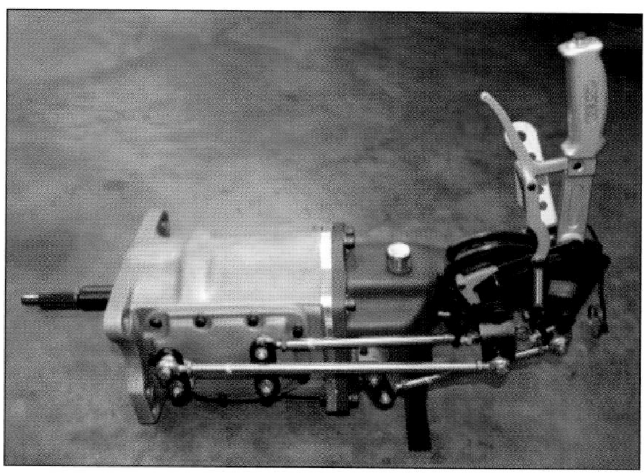
This is Long Shifters' high-tech vertical-gated shifter. By pulling the lever up, the shifter is positioned with the top gate. Releasing the lever allows the springs to pull the shifter's arm vertically down each gate and eliminates the need for a conventional H-pattern.

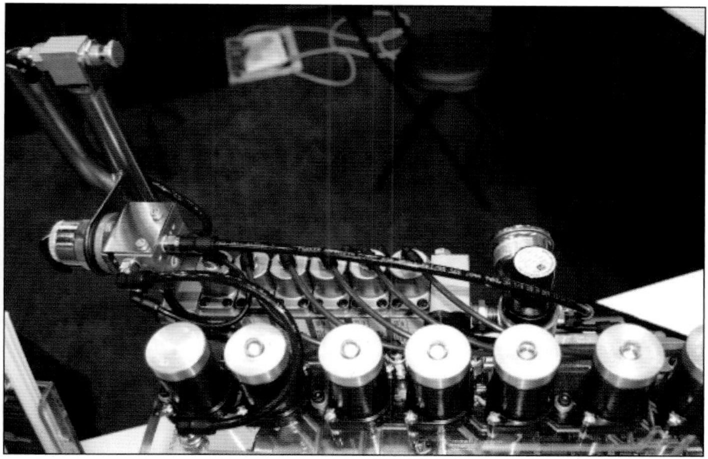
Jerico Transmission's air shifter has solenoid valves that route a high-pressure volume of air from one passage to another. A push-button actuates each shift, and a dial selects neutral or reverse.

The dotted line shows the path your 1/4-inch-diameter rod should take. The circle shows how the gates are aligned, but as you can see, they are not centralized within the shifter body. This is the only other way a shifter can cause a transmission to fall out of gear with a good neutral gate.

Sometimes in drag racing, the speed of your shift can make the difference between a win and a loss. These shifters were designed to create rapid shifts without the possibility of a "missed" shift.

Fixing the Hurst Competition Plus Shifter

There are more Hurst Competition Plus shifters floating around used and new than any other shifter around. By now, cleaning out the older units may be needed. These shifters, if properly maintained, never wear out. Hurst still sells typical bushings and clips in what they call a Pit Pack.

Oddly, many people don't understand what shifter adjustment will and will not do. There are only two adjustments that can be made with any conventional Hurst Competition Plus shifter. The first is a neutral gate adjustment, and the second is stop adjustment. If your transmission is falling out of gear and you have a good neutral gate (a clean left-to-right motion of the shifter), you can't turn any rods to eliminate that problem. Stop bolts can become loose and work themselves in too far. If the shifter falls out of gear, remove the stops and see if this resolves the problem. To align these shifters a 1/4-inch rod is pushed through the shifter body and the three gates. The rod aligns the gates with each other and centralizes the gates within the shifter body.

T5/T56 Shifter Modifications

The factory T5 shifter is simply a lever that pivots on a ball socket.

Side-to-side and forward-to-backward motions both ride on this ball socket. The centerline distance of your pivot-ball socket to the level end centerline determines the length of your throw. Until 2004, every aftermarket T5 shifter used the same principle. They just housed them differently, or used their own variations of bias spring pressures to come up with their own feel.

McLeod Industries' Red Roberts designed a pivot system using a vertically mounted spherical bearing.

Modifying a Hurst Competition Plus Shifter

1 Pry Apart Shift Body

With all the bolts removed, use a pair of drift punches and pry the shift body apart.

2 Unbolt Back Wall

Remove the back wall of the shifter body.

3 Remove Main Pivot Shaft

Remove the main pivot shaft by tapping it out or walking it out with a set of pliers.

4 Remove Gate Assembly from Shifter Body

Grasp the whole gate assembly and pull it out of the shifter body. Try to keep it together.

5 Inspect and Clean All Parts

Once out of the shifter body, carefully lay down each piece. You may want to clean each piece and return it to its proper place on the bench.

6 Verify Shifter Body Operation

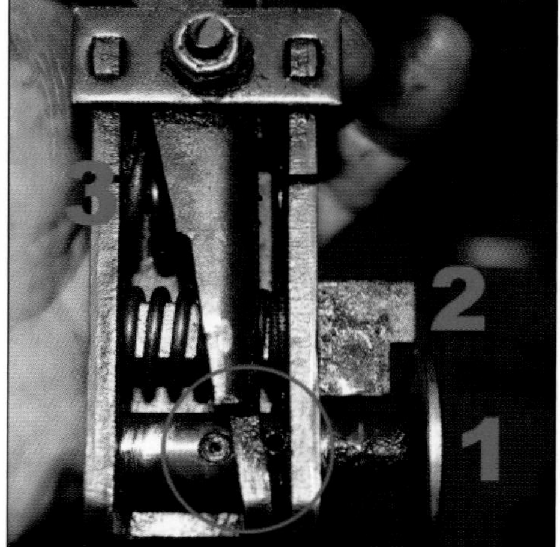

The plunger (1) basically contacts all three gates depending on how the shifter is biased left or right. The internal stop (2) is what gives you the extra effort to get into reverse. The spring (3) handles the normal left-to-right bias. The circle shows the roll pins that push the plunger left or right. The pin on the left broke, allowing the stick to move toward first gear, but not the plunger.

The Slik Stix shifter's design creates a very efficient geometry that produces shorter throws and narrower gates within a smaller package.

The T5 shifter is the most reproduced aftermarket shifter today. When it comes to the factory T5 shifter, there are no adjustments because it has only one internal shift rail, and an internal transmission track plate controls neutral. It becomes a shifter with very few components.

Hurst originally came up with a cast-alloy low-profile, short-throw shifter for Ford's SVO program. The shifter sparked interest from several companies to create billet shifters that didn't wear out as quickly. These sport billet-machined bodies with stop bolts. The stops keep the internal shift lugs from deforming under heavy load. Because factory T5 shifters are a non-serviceable item, I will show you how to modify the factory shifter for any specialized conversion you may have in mind.

Modifying the T5/T56 shifters in this manner makes for a clean-looking piece as opposed to some stick that is bolted on and spaced out in every direction possible. It also makes for a better-shifting assembly because the geometry is much more direct.

7 Replace Roll Pins

Replace the factory roll pins with solid, hardened pins available from any machine tool supply house. This is basically the only trick modification that needs to be done. Everything is cleaned. Reverse the above steps to assemble the shifter.

BONUS CONTENT:
Scan to learn how to rebuild a Hurst Competition Plus shifter.

Notice how the McLeod shifter uses a spherical bearing. This eliminates the need to keep the pivot loaded, prevents pivot wear, and allows for total spring bias adjustment with Bellville washers.

The low-profile shape of the McLeod Shifter also allows for many offsets without creating floor pan interference.

A stock T5 GM-style shifter is shown on the left, and a billet Steeda Tri-Ax shifter appears on the right.

Here is a wide variety of factory shifters that I keep to mix-and-match parts for various conversion projects.

Customizing a Stock T-5 Shifter

1 Cut Off Folded Section

Start to dismantle the T5 shifter by cutting off the rear folded section. Unfolding it and refolding will only weaken it, so just cut it off.

2 Disassemble Shifter Assembly

Tap the cover rearward with a hammer, and the whole shifter will come apart. Lift the stub assembly out of the socket base, and remember the order of the flat springs. Slide off the nylon ball.

Short-Throw and Normal-Throw Shifters

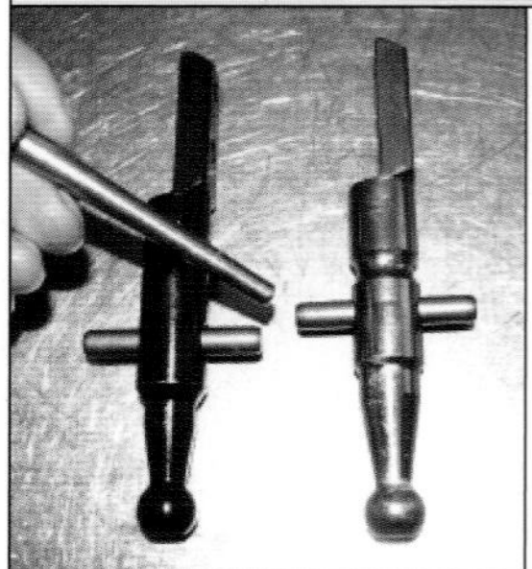

A normal-throw shifter stub is on the left, while a short-throw stub is on the right. They are the same length, but the position of the pivot shaft is higher on the short-throw version. The base is also higher on the short-throw shifter. You cannot mix bases and stubs, meaning a short-throw base stays with a short-throw stub.

3 Weld On New Shifter Fitting

Now start welding since all plastic parts and springs are removed. I'm welding a special fitting for my JT5 Jaguar shifter.

4 Create the Necessary Offset

The fitting creates the proper offset any angle for my conversion. You can do the same for any other conversion. The concept is the same.

5 Assemble Shifter

Assemble the shifter with all internal components greased. Clamp it together in a vise along with some Vise-Grips clamping the top half together with the base. It acts as a heat sink while the two halves are fuse-welded together. If you make a really long stick, add a couple of extra flat bias springs to get a better bias feel. Shifter internal parts are not available, so that is why I keep lots of shifters around.

6 Install Shifter Handle and Boot

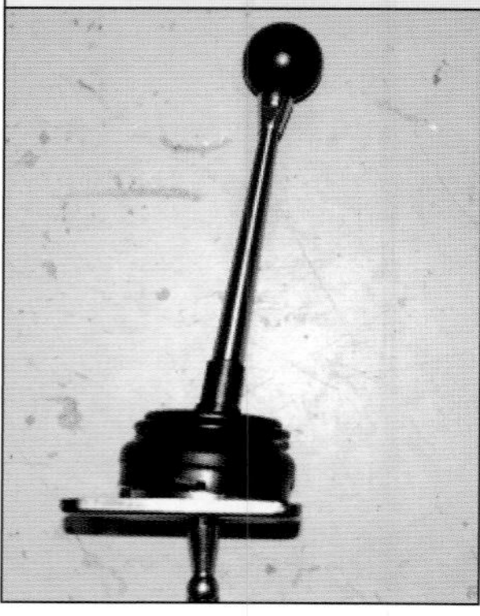

The fitting I weld on allows me to screw on my own custom stick, shift ball, and locking ferule.

Common General Motors Speedometer Gears

Part #	Description
345215	GM Speedometer Fitting with Seal
3708148	GM Hold-Down

Mainshaft Drive Gear (Still Available)

Part #	Tooth Count
3708144 8T	1.84-inch OD*
3708145 8T	1.76-inch OD*
3978758 8T	1.84-inch OD**

*Fits a 27-spline output shaft.
**Fits a 32-spline output shaft.

Mainshaft Driven Gear (Still Available)

Part #	Tooth Count
3987917	17T – Purple*
3987918	18T – Brown*
3987019	19T – Neutral/White*
3987920	20T – Blue*
3987921	21T – Red*
3987922	22T – Gray/Black*
3860345	22T – Green**
3860346	23T – Black**
3860347	24T – Yellow**
3860348	25T – Orange**
18-110-001	7T – 27-Spline Drive***
18-110-002	7T – 32-Spline Drive***

*Mates with the 1.84-inch drive gear.
**Mates with the 1.76-inch drive gear and is larger in diameter than the 1.84-inch-drive gears.
***Auto Gear has produced 7-tooth versions of the large-diameter versions of both spline speedo-drive gears.

Speedometer Gear Ratio Formulas

These formulas can be used to determine the proper speedometer-driven gear.

Speedometer Gear Ratio (SGR) = 63,360 x Axle Ratio ÷ 3,141.6 x Tire Diameter

Number of Driven Gear Teeth = SGR x Speedo Drive Tooth Count

Oil Types and Capacity

The Internet has created many online enthusiast forums for cars and transmissions. If you have visited one of these forums, at least a few times a week someone is asking about what oil type or brand they should use in their transmission. While there are many self-proclaimed experts in these forums, many do not provide reliable or accurate information. There has been a marketing hype by synthetic oil manufacturers claiming that the current 80W-90 API-GL5 oil corrodes bronze synchro rings. This may be true in theory, but after rebuilding thousands of transmissions, I have never seen this happen. Synthetics have a great deal of merit in cold climates. Transmissions, such as the Muncie, that don't have a front seal, usually end up leaking oil because synthetic oil flows better than conventional gear lube. In my experience, any 80W-90 or 75W-90 works well in the Muncie, T10, Super T10, and Toploader. The A833 Chrysler without bushed gears uses gear lube as well. The T5 and A833 with bushed gears use Dextron III-style lubricant.

People seem to be obsessed with oil capacity. None of the manual transmissions discussed in this book has a dipstick. Filling the transmission to the level of the fill plug determines the correct lubricant capacity. So the only reason you would need to know the capacity is to know how much oil you need to purchase. Transmissions, such as the T5 and A833, have different-length extension housings, and therefore capacity can vary within the same brand. Muncie and T10-style transmissions usually take 1¼ to 1½ quarts, while T5 and A833 transmissions accept close to 3 quarts. So if you pick up 3 quarts of oil, you'll probably be covered and have a little extra just in case you have a spill.

Torque Specifications

Muncie 4-Speed

Side Cover	18 ft-lbs
Front Retainer	25 ft-lbs
Extension Housing	30 ft-lbs
Speedo Hold-Down	10 ft-lbs
Fill/Drain Plugs	25 ft-lbs

T10 And Super T10

Side Cover	18 ft-lbs
Front Retainer	18 ft-lbs
Extension Housing	30 ft-lbs
Speedo Hold-Down	10 ft-lbs
Fill/Drain Plugs	25 ft-lbs
Mid Plate Bolt	30 ft-lbs

T5 5-Speed (NWC and WC)

Front Retainer	18 ft-lbs
Countergear Lock Plate	18 ft-lbs
Top Cover	10 ft-lbs
Shifter Base	18 ft-lbs
Extension Housing	25 ft-lbs
Fill/Drain Plug	25 ft-lbs
Hex Pivot	35 ft-lbs
Speedo Hold-Down	10 ft-lbs

Toploader 4-Speed

Top Cover	18 ft-lbs
Front Retainer	18 ft-lbs
Extension Housing	30 ft-lbs
Speedo Hold-Down	10 ft-lbs
3-4 Detent Bolt	20 ft-lbs
Fill/Drain Plug	25 ft-lbs

Chrysler A833 4-Speed

Side Cover	18 ft-lbs
Front Retainer	18 ft-lbs
Extension Housing	30 ft-lbs
Speedo Hold-Down	10 ft-lbs
Fill/Drain Plug	20 ft-lbs

Ratios at a Glance

Here is a quick guide to some of the popular and not-so-popular gear ratios.

Ford Toploader

1st	2nd	3rd	4th	
2.32	1.69	1.29	1.00	Close-ratio
2.78	1.93	1.35	1.00	Wide-ratio

Muncie 4-Speed

1st	2nd	3rd	4th	
2.20	1.64	1.28	1.00	M21/M22 Close-ratio
2.56	1.91	1.48	1.00	M20 Early Wide-ratio
2.52	1.88	1.46	1.00	M20 Late Wide-ratio
2.52	1.73	1.35	1.00	M21W Auto Gear Wide-ratio
2.56	1.75	1.36	1.00	M22W Auto Gear Wide-ratio
2.20	1.51	1.17	1.00	M22X Auto Gear Extra Close-ratio
2.20	1.51	1.00	0.86	M21Y Auto Gear Overdriveratio

T10 4-Speed (1957–1965)

Series	1st	2nd	3rd	4th	
T10	2.20	1.66	1.31	1.00	
T10A	2.54	1.92	1.51	1.00	
T10B	2.36	1.78	1.41	1.00	Ford
T10C	2.20	1.64	1.31	1.00	
T10D	2.54	1.89	1.51	1.00	
T10E*					
T10H	2.74	2.04	1.50	1.00	Ford
T10J	2.36	1.76	1.41	1.00	Ford
T10K**					
T10L	2.36	1.76	1.41	1.00	Ford
T10M	2.36	1.62	1.20	1.00	Ford Shelby
T10N	2.54	1.74	1.30	1.00	Aftermarket

*Same as T10D but with SAE 9310 gears
**Same as T10C but with SAE 9310 gears

Super T10 4-Speed (1st Design)

Series	1st	2nd	3rd	4th	
T10U	3.44	2.28	1.46	1.00	GM Truck
T10W	2.64	1.75	1.33	1.00	
T10S	2.43	1.61	1.23	1.00	
T10P	2.43	1.76	1.47	1.00	AMC
T10Q	2.64	2.10	1.60	1.00	FORD
T10T	2.64	2.10	1.46	1.00	AMC
T10V	2.23	1.77	1.35	1.00	AMC

Super T10 4-Speed (2nd Design Only)

Series	1st	2nd	3rd	4th	
T10W	2.64	1.75	1.33	1.00	
T10X	2.64	1.61	1.23	1.00	
T10Y	2.88	1.75	1.33	1.00	
T10Z	3.42	2.28	1.46	1.00	
T10AA	3.29	1.72	1.00	.80	Rare Overdrive Set
T10BB	4.17	2.28	1.46	1.00	
T10CC	2.88	1.91	1.33	1.00	GM Version

Saginaw 4-Speed

1st	2nd	3rd	4th
3.50	2.48	1.65	1.00
3.11	2.20	1.47	1.00
2.85	2.01	1.47	1.00
2.54	1.80	1.44	1.00

SOURCE GUIDE

Auto Gear Equipment
530 State Fair Boulevard
Syracuse, NY 13204
315-471-8141
315-471-8146 (fax)
www.autogear.net

Centerforce/Midway Industries, Inc.
2266 Crosswind Drive
Prescott, Arizona 86301
928-771-8422
928-771-8322 (fax)
www.centerforce.com

David Kee Toploader Transmissions, Inc.
San Antonio, TX 78266
877-276-8081
www.4speedtoploaders.com

5speeds.com
208 North US Highway 1, Unit #1
Tequesta, FL 33469
561-743-5600
561-741-7921 (fax)
www.5speeds.com

G-Force Transmissions
150 N. Grant Street
Cleona, PA 17042
717-202-8367
www.gforcetransmissions.com

Hurst Shifters
9142 Independence Avenue
Chatsworth, CA 91311
818-483-1366
www.hurst-shifters.com

Jerico Performance Products
443 Pitts School Road N.W.
Concord, NC 28027
704-782-4343
704-782-4443 (fax)
www.jericoperformance.com

Keisler Engineering
2250 Stock Creek Boulevard
Rockford, Tennessee 37853
USA
www.Keislerauto.com
888-609-0053 (toll free)
865-609-8187

Liberty's High Performance Products, Inc.
6390 Pelham Road
Taylor, Michigan 48180
313-278-4040
313-381-2411 (fax)
www.libertysgears.com

Passon Performance
309 Turkey Path
Sugarloaf, PA 18249
570-401-8949
www.passonperformance.com

Roltek Racing Transmissions
371 Prospect Avenue
Hartland WI, 53029
262-369-0490
262-369-0440 (fax)
www.roltektrans.com

R.T. Quaife Engineering Limited
Vestry Road, Otford,
Sevenoaks, Kent
TN14 5EL England
01732 741144
01732 741555 (fax)
www.quaife.co.uk

SK Speed
1075 Route 109
Lindenhurst, NY 11757
631-957-9427
www.skspeed.com

Steeda Autosports, Inc.
1351 NW Steeda Way
Pompano Beach, FL 33069
954-960-0774
954-960-1449 (fax)
www.steeda.com

Tilton Engineering
25 Easy Street
P.O. Box 1787
Buellton, CA 93427
805-688-2353
805-688-9407 (fax)
www.tiltonracing.com

TTC Automotive Tremec Transmissions
800-401-9866
734-456-3739 (fax)
www.ttcautomotive.com